From Ivory Tower to Academic
Commitment and Leadership

*Amalya is dedicating this book to her late parents, Tova and Haim Lumerman, with endless love.*
*Gili is dedicating this book to her babies, who bring her much pride, joy, and purpose.*

# From Ivory Tower to Academic Commitment and Leadership
The Changing Public Mission of Universities

Amalya Oliver-Lumerman

*Professor in the Department of Sociology and Anthropology, Hebrew University of Jerusalem, Israel*

Gili S. Drori

*Professor in the Department of Sociology and Anthropology, Hebrew University of Jerusalem, Israel*

Edward Elgar
PUBLISHING

Cheltenham, UK • Northampton, MA, USA

© Amalya Oliver-Lumerman and Gili S. Drori 2021

All rights reserved. No part of this publication may be reproduced, stored in a retrieval system or transmitted in any form or by any means, electronic, mechanical or photocopying, recording, or otherwise without the prior permission of the publisher.

Published by
Edward Elgar Publishing Limited
The Lypiatts
15 Lansdown Road
Cheltenham
Glos GL50 2JA
UK

Edward Elgar Publishing, Inc.
William Pratt House
9 Dewey Court
Northampton
Massachusetts 01060
USA

A catalogue record for this book
is available from the British Library

Library of Congress Control Number: 2020950925

This book is available electronically in the **Elgar**online
Business subject collection
http://dx.doi.org/10.4337/9781781000342

ISBN 978 1 78100 033 5 (cased)
ISBN 978 1 78100 034 2 (eBook)

Printed and bound by CPI Group (UK) Ltd, Croydon, CR0 4YY

# Contents

| | | |
|---|---|---|
| *Acknowledgements* | | vi |
| 1 | Introduction: academic commitment and leadership as a model for the 21st-century university | 1 |
| 2 | Public mission of universities: from ontology, to terminology, to strategy | 12 |
| 3 | The shaping of contemporary models for the university's public role: from CSR to ACL | 38 |
| 4 | Academic commitment and leaderships: types and examples | 64 |
| 5 | The Hoffman Leadership and Responsibility Programme at the Hebrew University: exemplar ACL community of practice within a university | 100 |
| 6 | ACL projects in an ACL-inspired programme: examples from the Hoffman programme | 121 |
| 7 | Concluding comments and reflections: new opportunities for university–society relations | 132 |
| *Bibliography* | | 147 |
| *Index* | | 160 |

# Acknowledgements

This book is inspired by, and stems from, Amalya's role as the designer, founder and co-director of Hoffman Leadership and Responsibility Programme at the Hebrew University in the years 2006–2020. It also draws on each of our ever-evolving research projects on universities: Amalya's studies of university–industry collaborations, knowledge production, networks and alliances in innovative sectors, corporate social responsibility and social entrepreneurship; and Gili's studies of the globalization of science and innovation, branding and managerialism in universities, and worldwide changes in higher education.

We are deeply appreciative of Sylvia and Harry Hoffman for their vision and the funding of the Hoffman Programme at the Hebrew University, Israel. We thank our research partners and many colleagues who, through our varied endeavors over the years to understand the university, shaped our ideas and opinions about this renowned institution, its history and its future. Our work here is also, obviously, influenced by our lives as academicians and our involvement in leading academic units and initiatives.

We are grateful for all these...

Amalya Oliver-Lumerman and Gili S. Drori
Tel Aviv, August 2020

# 1. Introduction: academic commitment and leadership as a model for the 21st-century university

Universities are undergoing dramatic changes – from exponential expansion of student enrolments and a proliferation of university foundings, to new technological means for teaching and research, to massive reforms of their governance and management – and such changes not only threaten the traditional view of the university as the prime knowledge organization but also reconfigure its relations with society. For decades, universities have been battling their image as the "ivory tower of academia", referring to elitist and insular organizations that are disconnected from society's challenges and needs. However, the university has a long history of engagement with society, which includes providing both the education and the forum to transform students into productive citizens as well as stimulating discoveries that have broadened human horizons.

The historiography of the university is, indeed, understood through the evolutionary process of the university's mission. The purpose of the university is informed by internal, institutional ambitions and by the external notion of the good life, and thus its transformation should be appreciated while keeping this duality of impetus in mind. Newer fundamental goals did not supplant the university's previous mission; rather, they emerged as new centres of purpose while integrating prior concerns as auxiliary to the mission. The university's mission metamorphosis began, at the outset, with the initial goal of teaching that defined the medieval university. The second mission, that of research, was introduced in the early 19th century to form the Humboldtian model of the university. Subsequently, a third mission of commercialization was introduced in the mid-20th century to create the entrepreneurial university.

During each of these epochal models of the university – a teaching organization, a knowledge-generating organization, and then also a productive organization – university–society relations were redefined.

Throughout the reformulations of the university's mission, and through generations of struggles to secure the autonomy of these institutions from political and economic pressures (while still reactive to these external stimuli as they inform the societal values *du jour*), universities have continuously been engaged with society, albeit it in different forms. Still, the spirit of 21st-century global society demands the university take on a new central aim: it requires that universities take social responsibility, adopt a leadership position, and have social impact.

These days, the language to describe a university's social role is changing worldwide, expressing a further responsibility of universities to expand their impact on society either economically, socially (broadly and thus ambiguously defined), or ecologically. Numerous indexes used to assess and compare universities have recently added dimensions that express the wish for universities to expand their impact on society. For example, several transnational initiatives are now organizations valorizing the social impact action of universities, thus setting academic commitment and leadership (ACL) to social causes as a normative and operational expectation. Two such initiatives were launched in 2019, spurring this normative change among both academicians and universities, on both the individual and organizational levels, while also encouraging the public to seek social yield from academic research. One is the European Commission's new Horizon Impact Award: research projects that received FP-7 or Horizon 2020 funding are eligible for additional recognition for the "use of their results to provide value for society". The second is the *Times Higher Education*'s new ranking of universities by their performance towards the social goals encoded as the United Nations' Sustainable Development Goals (SDGs). Our claims in this book are aligned with the spirit of these initiatives.

The demands upon universities to rethink their social role are captured in several iconic documents at every turning point. For instance, Vannevar Bush's 1945 *Science – The Endless Frontier* has been made sacred in expressing the economic commitments of universities towards the development of society's security and prosperity and thus the traditional "third mission" and "entrepreneurial university". Recently, such documents are emerging, delivering 21st-century expectations from the university. One such document is "The Communique of the 2009 World Conference on Higher Education", which was convened in Paris by UNESCO. This 2009 communique articulates these new challenges laid before universities; it unequivocally speaks of the social *responsibility* of higher education – that is, institutions and individuals alike. Decreeing this position, the document states the following:

> Faced with the complexity of current and future global challenges, higher education has the social responsibility to advance our understanding of multifaceted issues, which involve social, economic, scientific and cultural dimensions and our ability to respond to them. It should lead society in generating global knowledge to address global challenges, inter alia food security, climate change, water management, intercultural dialogue, renewable energy and public health. (Item 2)

With these words, the communique not only calls for academic responsibility but also expresses a sense of urgency due to the mounting challenges facing societies worldwide at the start of the 21st century. How are universities and academicians to respond to such expectations? How are they to balance societal expectations for scientific input with maintaining the core principles that secured the university's resilience over a thousand years? Therefore, what is the appropriate social role of universities under the new social conditions of the current era? The premise of our book is to suggest a path for securing the university's role as a socially engaged institution, expressing its social commitment, and taking its role as a leader towards social change. We therefore propose the model we call ACL – academic commitment and leadership – as the format for redefining the social role of universities and transforming university–society relations in a manner that befits our times.

## DEFINING ACADEMIC COMMITMENT AND LEADERSHIP (ACL)

In this book, we introduce, define, and analyse ACL. We argue that ACL, as implied by its title, reorients discussions of academia's social role and the impact of universities on the public good towards *commitment* and *leadership*. Therefore, the definition of ACL is a model for university–society relations that demands the socialization of academicians to pledge themselves to the advancement and protection of the public good, as well as stressing the importance of organizational reforms to facilitate this reorientation. ACL is constituted around three main themes:

1. Advancing the public good and social issues, allowing for a broad spectrum of targets and courses;

2. Fostering academic leadership of social impact and change, driven by both academicians and scientists as mainly a "bottom-up" process of responsibility and action; and
3. Institutionalizing structures and practices that encourage ACL and socialize new entrants into such a culture, yet also pertaining to the three existing missions of academia.

Together, the three defining elements weave a description of the goal (the public good), the actors (academicians), and the form (institutionalization of new norms with regards to the new mission). Importantly, this definition clarifies two distinct characteristics of ACL, compared with existing initiatives taken by universities and academicians to impact society. First, ACL's commitment to, and leadership of, social causes is distinct from the focus on economic or technological development, which stands firmly as the core of academia's third mission. Rather, as we define it, the proposed model of ACL orients academic commitment towards the advancement of the public good and social agenda and towards fostering leadership of social change as a distinct and integral goal of academic education (see Chapters 2 and 3). Second, ACL is driven by academicians and scientists; hence, it is mostly a bottom-up model for responsibility for the public good. Academia's leaders and managers should facilitate ACL by setting guidelines that encourage ACL themes and establishing programmes that enable ACL initiatives to flourish; nevertheless, ACL demands the socialization of academicians to pledge themselves to the advancement and protection of the public good. In this sense, although the engagement of universities with the societies in which they were and are embedded has old roots and many varieties, these university–society relations are predicated on the notion of the public (see Holmwood, 2011).

Seeing that the outlined ACL model relies on the initiatives of individual academicians, whereas universities are there to offer support and empower such activities, an important question is illuminated in stage lights: what is a socially responsible academic leader? We think that the definition of this hybrid identity is best explained by two concepts that originate from social network theories: "leveraging" and "brokerage".

Leverage is a positional advantage that provides power and ability to act effectively and influence people (Quinn, 1999; Quinn et al., 1996). In the context of ACL, leveraging refers to the ability of an academician to use the advantage associated with her or his reputable social position to create advantage in gaining certain socially oriented goals that she or he believes in and wishes to promote. Through leveraging, "ACL-ers" allow themselves to be associated with a public cause and to then steer attention and actions towards the advancement of this public cause. To create such an effect, the ACL-driven academician uses his or her reputation and renown as a scientist or academic official.

Brokerage, on the other hand, is a structural position that is able to bridge or bind two social domains that are otherwise disconnected (Burt, 2004, 2005). Being in such a brokerage position can benefit both the person in that position and the domains he or she connects: effective brokerage may bring great returns to the people occupying a brokerage position, as well as in terms of having them achieve their goals, and it may result in high innovation in the connected domains because of the transfer or crossing of ideas and practices between these otherwise distinct and separate social or organizational contexts (Burt, 2007). Therefore, for ACL and in general, brokerage position does not uniquely connect among individuals, but it can also connect between fields of action, social groups, organizational fields, and alike social entities. Through brokerage, an ACL-motivated academician harnesses resources from unconnected domains and enlarges the pool of possibilities by creating synergies and multiplication effects through the link he or she establishes. While leveraging and brokerage refer to the characteristics of the process and of the structure, respectively, jointly they have a powerful ability to call for public attention and lead to change. As strategic tools, they allow for a renowned academician to attract the needed attention and gather the needed resources to lead change by his or her ability to connect the academic world with the public or social needs. Overall, leveraging and brokerage allow an ACL-motivated academician to become a unique motivator and energizer of social attention and social change.

Reliant on these concepts-cum-strategies, ACL defines not only the actors for this renewed university – namely, academicians and universities, personas, and institutions – but also requires that their drive to impact the public good rests on both commitment and leadership – that is, on both will and action. Commitment refers to a dedication to the cause of having science and academia deliver a social import. Because, as elaborated on in Chapter 3, ACL is defined and strategized in reference to corporate social responsibility (CSR), the choice of the term "commitment" is made intentionally to distinguish our proposed ACL model from the term "responsibility". In the context of universities, the term "responsibility" not only connotes accountability, moral capacity and reliability but is also tied to university programmes – value-added innovations, commercialization, teaching service, and developmental impact – which we later define as capturing the third (rather than ACL and thus fourth) academic mission (see Geschwind et al., 2019, p. 4; Zhang et al., 2018). Therefore, for our discussions, commitment stands for a *sense of* obligation where academic activities should deliver social impact, alongside achieving academic and scientific excellence.

Leadership, in our use here, means taking the initiative to set an agenda, organize a project, and recruit and guide others to partake in it. Importantly, both are weaved together to make ACL inherent to the university and to academic being. To what causes should academia commit and in which direction should it lead? On that, we are agnostic. Following Derek Bok's (Bok, 1982) discussion on how a university might prioritize among social challenges that require its input or intervention, we too think that the university's core commitment is to the development of knowledge and that all other responsibilities and commitments are subservient to it. Still, as we elaborate on throughout the book and especially in Chapter 4, ACL has the power to infuse the established academic missions – of teaching, research, and commercialization – with new themes and practices. Like the addition of the second academic mission of research to the first mission of infused teaching with research-driven themes, and much like the introduction of the third academic mission of production and technology transfer that redirected the missions of teaching and research in new (and sometime contested) directions, we think that the adoption of ACL as a fourth academic mission, by both academicians and universities, will open new venues for university–society exchange and will best engage academia with contemporary social challenges.

Discussion of ACL is embedded in a longer tradition of analysing and commenting on the public role of universities. This rich scholarly field uses many different terms to describe similar ideas or concepts – of which we chose particular ones to serve as the more accurate descriptors of the meanings we see. First, which organizations do we refer to? What is the field or sector we refer to? For the sake of consistency and clarity, throughout this book, we rely on the term "universities". Indeed, this term is commonly paired with "mission" when considering the strategic orientation, planning, and public role of higher education and academia. Nevertheless, while discussions of missions specifically refer to universities, the dramatic expansion of higher education, which also means the dramatic growth in the number and types of organizations that are accredited to award academic degrees, challenges this labelling. Indeed, the field of higher education is currently populated by colleges, teacher colleges, and technical colleges and universities; these various categories have become regulated by whomever the national accreditation body is; and such categorization formally recognizes only universities as accredited to award doctoral degrees, from which the accreditation process proceeds to specification based on the accreditation of curricular programmes. The result is an "alphabet soup" of sorts – with academic accreditation that is so specific by degree and discipline or field that most academicians, let alone lay people, cannot identify: D.Phil. or PhD; and MA and MSc, with a bewildering array of additional disciplinary academic accreditations in MBA, MFA, MSW, MLIS, or MDiv.[1] There is one remedy to the confusion that results from the expansion and variation, and the accurate and most inclusive label for such variety is *higher education organizations*. However, the label of higher education organizations, or higher education institutions, orients the description towards education, sequencing with primary and secondary education and emphasizing teaching, learning, and skilling, whereas our intention is to comment on those organizations that are also committed to research and commercialization. Therefore, we employ the term "universities" to link our work with the scholarship on academic missions and to accentuate the plurality of academic missions in addition to teaching.

A second terminological choice that helps us maintain a conceptual focus throughout the book is specific to the naming of the academic missions. Alongside the well-encoded terms of "teaching" and "research" used to describe the first and second academic missions, discussions of the third academic mission commonly go under the title "entrepreneurial university". Enveloped in the term "entrepreneurial" are specific meanings that link the university to industry and to the production of knowledge that could be utilized for production and commercialization, and thus to technology transfer. However, these associations are not inherent to the notion of entrepreneurship; rather, entrepreneurship points more directly to the initiative and pursuit of social agents. Still, one of the claims that we advance in this book with regards to ACL is that initiative is central to the fourth mission; likewise, we argue that also inherent to ACL is that academic impact should reach outside the bounds of the university's gates. Therefore, to better articulate the defining features of the third mission and to differentiate it from ACL, which we advocate to be the fourth mission of universities, we herein refer to the third mission that is focused on *commercialization*. We find that this term best captures the third mission's orientation of the linear model of science–technology–

industrial use, and production. It also best captures the utilitarian connotation of academic knowledge.

Third, we wrestled with the term that describes the object, or target, of ACL: throughout this book, we claim that, like the third mission, ACL aims to have universities shatter their image as an insular "ivory tower" and engage with, and impact, other societal institutions. However, several terms are used to describe the non-commercial engagement of universities with societal institutions outside their bounds: universities' social role, universities' public role, or universities' drive to contribute to the public good. After long discussions, we settled on the phrase "public role" of universities, and we use it throughout the book to capture its address of civic and communal matters, and yet it allows us to distinguish ACL from the ambiguity of the term "social" that is inherent to the now-common practice of corporate social responsibility (CSR), which we describe as a referent category for ACL.

These terminological choices are a primer to our discussion of and claims regarding ACL. They allow us to engage with the abundant scholarship on university–society relations over the course of a millennium, while also setting an agenda for academic engagement with contemporary and future societal challenges. We write this book with both analytic and advocacy intentions: by analysing the history of the societal missions of universities and seeking the sources for their inspiration, we define ACL as an opportunity and a programmatic tool for universities worldwide to refine their goals in terms of the public good, declare their agency in conquering social challenges, and institutionalize this new model of university–society relations through new practices, structures, and behaviours that embody this newly defined fourth mission of the university.

## THEMES AND STRUCTURE OF THE BOOK

In this book, we ask the questions offered above in a way that is manifested in a combination of three main segments: evidence and examples, conceptual and analytical framing, and ideological advocacy and promotion. To provide evidence for emerging trends in the academic world, we collected a large sample of illustrative cases of what we term ACL (academic commitment and leadership), and we show evidence of some national and global processes that are associated with ACL. Towards the end of the book, we zoom into a specific site of ACL activities at the Hebrew University of Jerusalem, where the Hoffman Leadership and

Responsibility Programme was established and developed with the aim of creating a community of practice to generate a greenhouse for ACL. Throughout the book, we acknowledge the complexity and innovative nature of ACL that leads to areas of ambiguity and challenges of conceptual boundaries. While we understand that this is usually the nature of an emerging social paradigm, we aim to provide conceptual clarification and comparison of the framing of ACL to related paradigms. Our comparisons with other paradigms/missions go in two directions: an intra-institutional evolution (universities' historical perspective) and an inter-institutional evolution (comparison with CSR and influence of other societal dynamics). From an organizational and historical intra-institutional perspective, we provide an overview of the three established missions of universities – teaching, research, and production – and show how the emerging fourth academic mission of ACL compares with the long history of university–society relations. From an inter-institutional perspective, we compare between the CSR perspective in the for-profit organizational field to ACL in the academic field.

To design this ACL model and describe its principal features, we seek to engage with historical accounts of the university, discussions of publicness in organization studies, and studies of institutional dynamics of the organizational field of higher education. Overall, we draw on several fields of scholarships, on many tales of ACL-like initiatives and programmes from universities worldwide, and on the 14-year experience of the first author in leading an ACL doctoral programme at the Hebrew University of Jerusalem, namely the Hoffman Fellowship Programme.

Following this Introduction, Chapter 2 describes the historic roots of academia's public role. In this chapter, we review the frequently cited historiography of universities, which describes this institution's millennium of persistence as a sequence of responses to changing social conditions by adding academic missions. We then situate this historiography in a polemic essay about publicness, discussing how the general debate of university–society relations transmuted into a contemporary scheme for the higher education sector.

Chapter 3 seeks out sources for this more recent demand that universities express social responsibility. We argue that contemporary discussions of universities' social import and impact are translations of CSR models into academia. As universities are redefined as organizations – that is, formal, complex, and managed entities – and thus borrow governance models from other sectors, academia is also using CSR as a form of reference for its relations with society. We propose that ACL, while driven by CSR legitimacy, offers a model that is relevant to the longstanding, even ever-changing, public role of universities.

Chapter 4 offers an analytic description of ACL practices, describing types of ACL and examples for them. Our examples combine tales about universities and academicians: academic leaders – Einstein as an illustrative example – who are renowned scientists using their academic reputation to establish ACL attitudes, which later institutionalized as iconic models, and academic organizations, which institutionalized programmes and procedures that deliver ACL principles.

Chapter 5 outlines how the ACL model is and can be implemented for a university, arguing that ACL requires the constitution of an ACL-inspired academic community of practice. After describing the main features of a community of practice, we exemplify how team-building and establishing the normative culture became integrators that enhanced ACL practices. Due to the personal involvement of Oliver-Lumerman, the first author, in the founding and designing of a specific programme for ACL, Chapter 5 describes the Hoffman Leadership and Responsibility Programme that was established at the Hebrew University. It is a fellowship programme for excellent doctoral students from all disciplines that was dedicated to ACL through the facilitation of a community of practice. The characteristics of the programme, as well as the group processes that were facilitated, are described in Chapter 5.

Together, Chapters 5 and 6 offer confirmation for ACL practices: both on the organizational level, including organizational processes, and also on the individual level of academicians, we provide more in-depth illustration. Following Chapter 5, Chapter 6 celebrates a series of ACL-inspired projects at the Hoffman programme. With that, we provide inspiring examples of programmes, initiatives, and targets in the hope that these will serve as inspiration for future ACL initiatives. Chapter 6 provides examples of ten ACL projects that were developed by doctoral fellows of the Hoffman programme. These projects show the wide spectrum of cases where academic knowledge and understanding can be translated to societal needs in various directions.

Chapter 7 summarizes our arguments regarding ACL as the fourth mission of the university, also immersing them in discussions of the character and history of academia – central among them are the issues of autonomy and "academic freedom". In this chapter, we also *advocate* for ACL: we confess that aside from our analytic interest in institutional changes to universities, we also believe that ACL is an important mission for universities. Here, we let our "bias" show in the hope of directing our home institution and colleagues away from the prediction of the managerialist doom of academia, anticipating that the "real" fourth mission of universities is promotional, and towards accepting a fourth academic mission that harnesses the university for the expansion of the public good.

Overall, our book seeks to combine a description of the normative-cum-programme that is already budding in today's universities with the advocacy of ACL as a strategic and actionable model for 21st-century universities. Today, yet again, questions about the future of universities are raised: is the university still a relevant social institution and, if so, how? Are academicians disconnected from "real life" and thus becoming irrelevant? Also, can universities keep up with the pace of social change and the magnitude of global society's grand challenges? We respond to such questions by offering our interpretation of which direction academia is moving these days and where it should proceed and expand to better articulate university–society relations in vision and in action.

## NOTE

1. For the sake of not overshadowing the claim regarding the proliferation of academic degrees by these undecipherable acronyms, we add here a dictionary of sorts: Master of Business Administration (MBA), Master of Fine Arts (MFA), Master of Social Work (MSW), Master of Library and Information Studies (MLIS), and Master of Divinity (MDiv).

# 2. Public mission of universities: from ontology, to terminology, to strategy

Derek Bok, former president of Harvard University, begins his canonized book *Beyond the Ivory Tower* (2009) with a quote from the previously canonized book *The Uses of the University* by Clark Kerr (1963/2001), former president of the University of California. In this passage, Kerr seeks explanations for the persistence of the institution of the university and for its continuous privilege since the Middle Ages and up until our current age. He wrote,

> What is the justification for the modern American multiversity? History is one answer. Consistency with the surrounding society is another. Beyond that, it has few peers in the preservation and dissemination and examination of eternal truths: no living peers in the search for new knowledge; and no peers in all history among institutions of higher learning in serving so many of the segments of an advancing civilization. (Kerr, quoted in Bok 2009, p. 1)

Indeed, the resiliency of the millennium-old organizational form of the university, as the site for advanced learning and development of knowledge, is evidence of the university's meaningful role for society. *What is this public role of the university?* The answer to this question has been open to public debate for several generations and suggesting an answer to this question – and an answer that befits our era – is the goal of our book.

Universities have been battling the impression that they are an "ivory tower", aloof from societal quotidian needs and conditions by their privilege in the pursuit of knowledge. To challenge this impression, universities are increasingly vocal about their claimed engagement in, involvement with, and even contribution to society. Here lies the conundrum: on the one hand, the social role of universities is a taken-for-granted premise for societies worldwide, whereas, on the other hand, universities are repeatedly called to justify the public's confidence in their utility as centres of knowledge production and education.

Nevertheless, for people on both sides of this debate about the social role of universities, the discussion centres on the scope and target of their mission rather than on the very existence and feasibility of academic higher education and research. In the current era, academia, research universities, and other tertiary education organizations are perceived as partners to the creation of the public good and its distribution. Much like hospitals' role regarding public health and the military's role regarding public security, the social role of universities is rooted in their participation in, if not responsibility over, the public sphere that is oriented towards the public's good and reliance on the public's legitimacy. The definition of public responsibility, which has seeped into private and for-profit organizations over the past several decades, has become the informal obligation of every contemporary organization: "The arrival of empowered organizational actorhood", argue Pope et al. (2018, p. 1301), "has precipitated a concomitant, cross-sectoral movement toward organizational social responsibility." Universities, which have been described as public institutions in a broad and varied sense, are therefore wrestling now not only with their legacy of relations with society over their long history, but also with the current institutionalization of social responsibility as a feature of any and all organizations. The ideas we bring forth in this book are aimed at problematizing this discussion of social or public commitment by examining academia and universities. By shedding an institutionalist light onto the longstanding debate about the public role of universities, we highlight the importance of examining, if not demanding, the idea that universities should assume social responsibility within its social context.

## THE ONTOLOGY OF SOCIAL COMMITMENT

A common phrase used during our times to describe the so-called "social contract between organizations and the society" in which they are embedded is social responsibility. Commonly attached to corporations, the term "corporate social responsibility" (CSR) came to represent the contract between corporations and society at large. Specifically, regarding corporations, the term, as well as the many forms of corporate strategy formulated to activate this agenda, emerged to describe the resolution of the tension between the profit motive of corporations, on the one hand, and the public good or the commons, on the other hand. With regards to organizations in general, the idea captured in "social responsibility" is the engagement of the given organization with its society or community, and it describes such engagement as one of responsibility – meaning an obligation to care for, contribute to, and be accountable for society. Such common understandings are rooted in an ontology of the social contract, which assumes a contractual (formal or informal) bond among members of a society and between organizations and their society. Explicated by political philosophers, most notably John Rawls, who himself drew upon the works of Thomas Hobbes, John Locke, and Jean-Jacques Rousseau, such a contract or bond depends on three conditions: it assumes public reason and some sort of consent; it reflects the socially legitimate definition of justice; and it sets the basis for cooperation and traditionally also for political association (see Bok, 2009; Nyborg, 2003). With these, the ontological basis of discussions about society members' social responsibility is quintessentially modernist in tone.

This modernist world of meanings saturates the institutionalized discursive link between the university and its social or public role. The role, described as public commitment or the public mission of the university, frames the university related to its social context, which is widely defined. University–society relations may be debated – that is, how separated or engaged universities are; what kinds of contributions universities make towards society; and so on – but are nevertheless immersed in discourse about relations and boundaries. On the one hand, universities and the society in which they are embedded are bound by relations of exchange, contribution, and sponsorship. Or, on the other hand, such relations reify the boundedness of each, calling attention to the recurring disputes over academic autonomy, political intervention, funders' influence, and social needs. In the following section, we unpack these ontological foundations for the taken-for-granted discussion of universities' social role and responsibility by discussing the meanings conveyed in the phrases and terms commonly used to describe it. The goal of the following discussion is to problematize the various phrases and terms and to draw from it a terminology that most conveys our approach.

By unpacking the part of the phrase that addresses the universities' commitment, multiple terms are used to describe such a commitment. The term "responsibility" is used most commonly, which implies custodial charge or conscious care and duty (Geschwind et al., 2019). This term, however, is most strongly associated with the recent turn in business ethics towards CSR; and, as we describe in more detail in the following chapters, it is as an extension of CSR that the term is now frequently applied to other organizations, as well as to universities.

Second, the term "role", as in "social role", implies a more neutral position as to the relations between the university and society. From a sociological perspective, this term refers to expectations: the social role, here of universities, is defined by the normative beliefs and prospects of the society or community in which the university is embedded and operates.

Third, the term "mission" is most commonly used by scientists themselves, conveying the meaning that the obligation of universities to society is a professional calling, obligation, and purpose, as captured in Weber's idea of *beruf*. Albert Einstein and José Ortega y Gasset are the most well-known scientists to have invoked the terminology in their reflection about the public mission of the 20th-century university: Einstein titled his public letter, published on the occasion of the opening of the Hebrew University of Jerusalem in 1925, "The Mission of Our University" (see Chapter 4), and Ortega y Gasset titled his series of 1930 lectures at the University of Madrid, reflecting on the role of higher education in liberal democracy, *Mission of the University* (1946/2002). Historiographers of universities and academia have also used the term "mission" to describe the fundamental goal that has defined and redefined since the foundation of the first university in medieval Europe over a thousand years ago. As described in detail in the following section, the history of universities is described as a linear, however punctuated, progression of three modes of the university, each defined by a mission – from the model of the medieval university whose sole mission was teaching, to the Humboldtian 19th-century university model whose mission pivoted to focus on research, and to the entrepreneurial university model of the mid-20th century whose mission concentrates on social contribution. This historiography shows that this long process is related not only to the definition of knowledge and to the process of knowledge creation but also to the usability of university knowledge. In summary, the responsibility, role, or mission of the university is related to the ways through which a university's so-called outputs are used by the public outside the bounds of the university. While there are numerous terms used to describe the nature of such a relationship between society and the university – obligation, engagement, partnership, collaboration, dialogue, service, and more – two emerge as most dominant: the term "responsibility", which conveys the idea of duty, and the term "mission", which conveys a sense of commitment.

Who are the beneficiaries of such an academic mission? Who are the "impactees" of the university's drive to deliver social impact? Attached to these notions of responsibility or commitment are, commonly, the terms "social" and "public". Still, much like the arguments over the terminology of responsibility/mission, the use of this or that term to describe these recipients of the university's good is likewise telling of one's ontological perspective. Here, too many terms are used interchangeably, although they each convey a unique meaning. For example, "community" conveys a sense of an intimately woven and not necessarily formally organized society, whereas "civic" conveys a sense of nongovernmental, not-for-profit, communal, and possibly volunteer constituency. Often, especially in regard to specific initiatives and policies, the university is linked with a specific sector – commonly government, industry, or business. At other times, the university is linked to more abstract affiliates or beneficiaries such as the environment or humanity. In addition, meaning regarding the directionality of the relationship is also enveloped in the use of "beneficiaries" and "recipients" rather than "partners" or "stakeholders". While many similar terms are used to describe the goals of universities, only two are commonly a part of the coined phrase. Of these, "social" conveys a general approach to all things social (e.g., economic, cultural and political, local, or global), whereas "public" conveys the meaning of a sphere open to all, often associated with open discussion and thus the commons.

Overall, whether we speak of "academia" or "science" or specifically note "the university", discussions regarding these institutions are linked, for centuries, with discussions of the public good. In this regard, discussions of the social role of universities and thus the social commitment of universities are related to other discussions of the public good and the commons. Likewise, the current challenges, not to say assaults, on academia and the university – for becoming increasingly more expensive for students and their families, for not providing training that is relevant for labour market placement, for parochial political views, or the like – are equally related to discussions about the so-called tragedy of the commons, where self-interestedness and shared interests come into conflict. Several contemporary debates exemplify this tension inherent to the university's expansive public mission.

Most archetypal in this regard is the debate around proprietary rights to knowledge developed in university labs, mainly in the life sciences (see, for example, Etzkowitz, 2003; Gulbrandsen and Smeby, 2005; Rhoten and Powell, 2007). These days, universities bargain with their faculty members over the share of ownership of proprietary knowledge, where universities take the side of responsibility for the public's benefit, whether in open access to this knowledge or in reclaiming a proportional share of the profits gained through the public's so-called investment in the development of that knowledge; even in private universities, such bargaining is done under the terminology of "the public", where the community is defined as a small circle of stakeholders. In such cases, which we will come to discuss at length later in the book, claims for the public mission of universities are anchored in the ethos of the university. Also, importantly, such claims reflect different traditions of justification.

## WHAT'S BETWEEN THE UNIVERSITY AND PUBLIC COMMITMENT? FOUR PERSPECTIVES

Research and commentary on the social role, or commitment, of public institutions can be divided into four streams: law, economy, justice, and culture. Each stream reflects a distinct intellectual and disciplinary approach as well as a distinct tradition of justification.

First, from a legal perspective, a public institution is a legally recognized entity, and therefore its social or public role is a core component of its certification and registration as such. Applied to universities, a legalistic approach would stipulate that a university's public role is derived from its accreditation as a statutory body, be it publicly or privately owned, and by its recognition as such by the law of the land. Therefore, over and above their academic accreditation, universities worldwide are also registered as a legal entity – that is, a not-for-profit association, for-profit company, or whatever the legal framework is at any given jurisdiction. Such registration facilitates their legal obligations regarding, for example, ownership, access, and employment.

From this perspective, the public role of universities is anchored in laws and regulations, which also define the public as well as the rights and obligations of an organization to the public. One such example is the legal prohibition of discrimination in most national constitutions, which shapes the policy and criteria of universities within that national legal jurisdiction regarding student admissions, student financial aid, faculty employment, and knowledge dissemination. In such cases, beyond the national legal framework specifically addressing prejudice-free education, universities are bound to conform with norms and regulations that in general define the public and set provisions for civil relations of organizations with the public. As a result, universities not only write their own rules and regulations, which specify the university's public and its obligations to it, but are also placed within multiple – often nested and occasionally conflicting – legal regimes that conceptualize both the public and the mission. In federal nation-states, such as Canada, the United States, and Germany, the rules and regulations of each university are nested within the state's specific regulations regarding education and higher education. These regulations are nested within the state's statutes and constitutions, which are themselves settled within the federal or national statutes, laws, and constitution. At the same time, universities are bound by agreements with partner organizations – universities, funding agencies, and corporations – which may traverse these legal jurisdictions and further prescribe the university's autonomy to define its public mission. In this sense, the legal aspects of universities' increasingly complex governance structure serve as a prism for defining the university's public mission.[1]

Second, from an economic perspective, the public role of universities is measured by the economic return on investments in education and research. This means that financial support for higher education and science comes from public budgets with the expectation of future, however indirect, yield for the public as a whole. The expectation is that economic return or yield would come to individual people, firms and agencies, and nations and humanity. Economic benefits are expected for the people who acquired higher education and training or whose research has commercial applications; those organizations that harness human capital and technology, which originated in universities, towards their productive goals; and, by extension, national and global economies. Also, such benefits, while all falling under the heading of "economic", refer to a variety of so-called returns: financial (royalties, yields, and funding), industrial (start-ups and spin-off firms, collaborations with corporate R&D, and tech transfer), commercial (sale of products of research), or human capital related (skilling and professional accreditation). This marketized approach also assumes rationality and calculability, competition and efficiency, and, thus, choice: it regards all matters pertaining to higher education and the university, such as access and cost, as it relates not only to public funding choices but also to individuals' life choices.[2]

Third, taking a justice perspective navigates any discussion of the university's public role towards the issue of its position in the distribution of social resources. From this perspective, the university's social commitment is directly related to notions of distributive justice, social mobility, and equal use of the general goods of education and erudition. In addition, the university's social obligation also extends to more specific utilities that stem from professional credentialing or the use of technologies that were developed through academic research. The lead concerns are with the public's accessibility to scientific and academic arenas, which were until recently reserved solely for the social elite. Note the two strands of public goods. For one, following the *Bildung* philosophical tradition that highlights self-improvement and self-cultivation of human capabilities (see Levin and Greenwood, 2016; Løvlie and Standish, 2002), widely accessible academic education and erudition set the necessary basis for modernization and for democratic, or otherwise participatory, politics.

In addition, following a more utilitarian approach, widely accessible academic credentialing and tech-based outputs directly influence life chances and well-being, and academic education provides not only social capital but also network ties for future employment. University-based research projects, in fields ranging from pharmaceutical to defence, to communications, are "triply helixed" with the industry and the government to generate regional and national development. These all offer an exposure to a wide range of contacts and networks as well as capabilities. For both strands, the implied definition of the public is very wide, addressing all social strata and groups (see Levin and Greenwood, 2016). Importantly, in general terms, universities are a part of the civilizational project: most loudly, Clark Kerr (1963/2001) proclaimed that the university is the driving force of modernity and is a foundational element in modern society.

Last, from a cultural perspective, the very discussion of the commitment of public institutions, including the university, is deeply rooted in modernity – that is, in the Western, now global, culture. In this cultural context, references to the social role or "public mission" of the university reflect core normative principles – that is, that organizations are members of communities and that communities coalesce around, or are defined by, a mutual commitment. Such normative principles are formally prescribed in the now-common organization practices of "vision–mission–goal" statements.

These formal organizational documents, as well as the many forms of CSR initiatives (which are described further in subsequent chapters), are pronouncements of adherence to the norms of the shared public sphere. Importantly, the very definition of the organization or sector is predicated upon its commitment to its community, thus also blurring the boundary between so-called public and private organizations. In the field of public policy, such public commitment is captured in the term "publicness"; Bozeman (1987, 2013) defined this paradigm as scaled between publicness and privateness and the axes of economic authority and political authority.

On such a grid, the university would score high on publicness towards society in general, with relatively high political publicness and with more pronounced economic publicness among private universities. Publicness is more than a utilitarian strategy of engagement in order for the university to maintain public legitimacy and support, which itself reveals the normative context that privileges public engagement as a basis for social reward. Rather, from this perspective, universities' normative commitment to publicness is driven by a *beruf*-like dedication to commitment. In institutional-phenomenological terms, which seek out the implied meanings in everyday practices, the normative dedication to publicness is a matter of social role: publicness constructs "roleness", specifying the role to be predicated on public commitment.

Overall, the four perspectives on the social role or commitment of public institutions reveal the formidable, however diverse, consensus on the important social contract between organizations that are considered public and the communities or societies in which they reside. Moreover, unlike the notion of CSR – which, as we argue in the following chapter, has been increasingly taken for granted and is no longer problematized as camouflaging the contradiction between corporations' private and profit motives and their ability to care for the public good – the idea of a university's social commitment is hardly ever contested. Notwithstanding private for-profit universities (such as the American Phoenix University) or the marketized and promotional impulses of a university's professional schools (such as business schools; see Gioia and Corley, 2002), universities are actually taken to "be good" rather than merely "look good".

Although the share of private universities among higher education institutions is largely growing, even private or for-profit universities are acknowledged as bound to a social contract with society at large and with their immediate community. In this regard, social commitment is a constitutive myth of academia and of universities, and the social role of academia and universities is very rarely contested. Moreover, interestingly, none of these four defining perspectives of universities' social role negate the commitment to academia's autonomy (see the discussion by Tapper and Salter, 1995). Rather, from either perspective, and using whatever logic governing the definition of academia's publicness, universities have reserved the privilege of sovereign responsibility for their judgment and knowledge and the privilege of self-government, which are captured in the term "autonomy". This idea of the university's autonomy has changed over the thousand-year history of its institution – and, most importantly, it had never meant self-sufficiency – but it has served as a constitutive ethos for universities throughout history and worldwide.

## THE HISTORIOGRAPHY OF UNIVERSITY: THREE MISSIONS, TWO REVOLUTIONS

The organizational form recognized as a university is soon to celebrate its thousand-year anniversary; the founding of the first recognized universities occurred in 11th-century Europe. This sets the university as a most unique and thus interesting case for the study of knowledge production and organizational continuity. Inquiring after the terms that enabled the European university model to survive over the course of many centuries and social changes, historiographers of the university overwhelmingly agree on the course of its change (see, for example, Grant, 1984; Nowotny et al., 2001; Riddle, 1993; Wissema, 2009). They describe the very long history of the university as punctuated by two academic revolutions and thus divided into three eras. These historiographers define each era by the university's mission, or normative goal, and conceptualize each revolution at the demarcating points wherein the university adopts a new mission.

The founding of the University of Bologna in 1088 and its official charter of 1558 mark the creation of the university, defined as an institution of advanced studies that is formally accredited to award academic degrees. The exact timing of this event and of the founding events that followed are obscured by myth and competition, with historical records differentiating between dates of founding and dates of being awarded a royal charter. Nevertheless, the founding of the European model of higher learning, which took the form of a *studium generale*, soon materialized with the founding of a series of medieval universities; following the University of Bologna, the founding of the universities of Paris, Oxford, Vicenza, Cambridge, Valencia, Salamanca, and others soon accumulated so that 20 universities were established by the year 1300, 20 additional universities by 1400, and a total of 70 universities across Europe by 1500. The emergence and institutionalization of the European university model in the Middle Ages imprinted the Western – now global – intellectual, political, economic, and technological society (Colish, 1997).

While medieval universities varied by areas of study and reputation, they all shared a few defining features. Prominent among them is the focus on higher learning, thus defining the first mission of the university as teaching. This focus is reflected in the structure and practices at these institutions. As a structural embodiment of this mission, universities of this era commonly included four faculties: theology, law, medicine, and arts. Importantly, the canonization of this foursome of disciplines is rooted in three criteria: the religious character of each discipline, its social utility, and its intellectual dignity (Verger, 1992, p. 42). Not precluding conflicts over the universal validity of these criteria and thus over the formalization of these four disciplines, the mission of teaching was also expressed in the ideal of the *bios theoretikos*, which gives precedence to the contemplative search for truth for its own sake, over the *bios praktikos*, which "gives precedence to social utility in the application of scientific knowledge and in the professional training provided by universities" (Rüegg, 1992, p. xxvii). It is this ethos that differentiated the medieval European university from the Roman, Islamic or Chinese schools that preceded it.

Universities were also privileged by their incorporation as autonomous entities, guaranteed in their charter, which allowed for expanded intellectual and operational autonomy and for greater student and faculty liberties. While medieval universities remained at the service of God and the church (Djelic, 2012, p. 100), their autonomy and liberty were expressed, for example, in the universal classification of students and faculty. University licenses, or *licentiate docendi*, entitled their holder to teach throughout Christendom (Verger, 1992, p. 36), thus enabling self-government and mobility, creating a trans-local academic community, and fortifying the ethos of the universality of knowledge and scholarship. Such normative cohesion of the medieval university model, which served to harmonize exchange among otherwise diverse forms of structure and operations, also meant the shared focus on teaching and learning. For example, the development of pedagogies, which persists until today, fosters learning though "lecture" (giving students mastery of authoritative knowledge) and "dispute" (debating to defend a doctrinal "case" or thesis), and it reveals the extent to which teaching was *the* defining mission for the community and network of medieval universities.

The rapture that is the first academic revolution, and which marks the addition of research as the second mission of the university, is the Enlightenment and the rise of the nation-state. As a part of the civilizing ideals of the new regime, from the early 18th century and on, the university emerged as a vehicle for the constitution of the nation-state. The new regime, inspired by the Enlightenment and formulated by Westphalian ideals, called for a new form of knowledge and scholarship, validated through research. The quintessential leader of this first academic revolution is Wilhelm von Humboldt (1767–1835), who proclaimed the role of universities as the pursuit of such new form of research-generated knowledge.

> [It should be] a special feature of the higher scientific establishments that they treated science as a problem that is never completely solved and therefore engaged in constant research. (Humboldt, quoted in Djelic, 2012, p. 101)

In this way, the first academic revolution added to the primary mission of teaching the second academic mission – that is, of conducting research that follows the scientific method of experimentation, disclosure, and rationality. In its focus on research-based science, the Humboldtian university model continues the tradition of the medieval university's quest for knowledge through investigation. Yet, most importantly, the Humboldtian university model marries the academic missions of teaching and research, prescribing that such a union of teaching and research is archetypically a humanist principle. Acting upon his ideals and building upon his stature as a philosopher, minister, and diplomat, Wilhelm von Humboldt founded the University of Berlin in 1810, which has since been renamed Humboldt University of Berlin, after his naturalist brother Alexander von Humboldt and himself. Humboldtian ideals and the related features of the new university were carried forth and spread beyond Europe by the structuration of the nation-state worldwide. For example, the founding of "land grant universities" in 19th-century US by the Morrill Acts of 1862 and 1890, as well as the subsequent bequeath of federal lands to US states, prescribed the teaching of practical science, agriculture, and engineering (even if "without excluding other scientific and classical studies"), while more generally aiming to reconstitute the American nation following the Civil War and to lead it through the industrial revolution.

Likewise, the creation of a Jewish university was on the agenda of the first Zionist Congress of 1897 and was decided on during the 11th Zionist Congress of 1913, leading to the foundation of the Hebrew University of Jerusalem in 1925. As such, the German and then American cultural and political hegemonies are responsible for the subsequent and worldwide popularity of the model of the Humboldtian University. For the centrality of serving the state and nation in the ethos of universities during this second era of the institution's history, Marie-Laure Djelic (2012) named this university model "the Westphalian university", thus referencing the series of peace treaties of the 17th century that constituted the notion of sovereignty. These gave rise to the modern nation-state and described this university model as one that "placed a Humboldtian structure in the service of each nation (in construction or consolidation)" (p. 101).

Following World War II, and in light of the principles set by Vannevar Bush for science to be harnessed for furthering development and security, the university model experienced a second academic revolution, resulting in what Kerr (1963/2001) labelled "the entrepreneurial university". Since the mid-20th century, universities grew in number and scope to become globally institutionalized (Frank and Meyer, 2020; Ramirez and Meyer, 2013; Schofer and Meyer, 2005), but also, importantly, they incorporated a third academic mission, adding economic transactions, industrial contacts, and social development to the prior missions of teaching and research. In practical terms, the second revolution is associated with emerging entrepreneurial activities and technology transfer, thus intertwining economic development with the first two missions of universities. Consequently, in spite of the subsequent critique, Burton Clark's 1998 book and his notion of the "entrepreneurial university" has gained prominence worldwide, taking strong hold in both research and policy (see Rhoades and Stensaker, 2017) and recognized as a global model (Pinheiro and Stensaker, 2014).

This revolution capitalizes on knowledge and focuses on technology transfer and the commercialization of inventions resulting from university research so as to bring products of research innovation to the market for the direct and indirect benefit of the public. There exist numerous forms of commercialization of academic knowledge, including IP patenting, licensing activities of intellectual property (IP), university–industry technology transfer, university spin-offs, and various forms of collaboration with the industry over efforts to commercialize scientific inventions by the university. It is argued that in order to present the benefits of inventions resulting from university research, it is the mission of universities to advance patenting and technology-transfer activities (see Kretz and Sá, 2013; Mowery et al., 2004; Perkmann et al., 2013; Shore and McLauchlan, 2012). These various practices that link the university and industry become the main vehicle through which inventions, such as new drugs, technologies, or innovative products, can be commercialized for the general benefit of society (Oliver and Liebeskind, 2009).

This approach models and depicts innovation processes as resulting from collaborative efforts among the university, government, and industry, as these are captured by the triple helix model (Etzkowitz and

Leydesdorff, 2000). The triple helix model is exemplified by Stanford University and MIT: these icons of the "third generation university" (Wissema, 2009) demonstrate the role of universities in the digital revolution, the regional development of Silicon Valley and Route 128, and the global high-tech boom. The imprint of these idealized entrepreneurial universities is visible in the adoption of, for example, technology-transfer offices in universities in various countries (see, Krücken, 2003; Krücken et al., 2007). Henry Etzkowitz further explained that the transition from the second to the third era is not as simple as a change from the Humboldtian university model to the entrepreneurial university model. Rather, he illustrated (see Figure 2.1) that the change in universities' mission orientation depended on both the degree of independence from the state and the degree of interaction with other spheres, thus also accounting for the expanding variety of university models during the 20th century. These various models are, in essence, differentiated by the type and depth of their engagement with the society in which they are embedded. Importantly, these interconnections and thus interdependencies between the university and its industrial, commercial and governmental partners drive both horizontal and vertical accountability in universities and form networked mode of governance (Jongbloed et al., 2008).

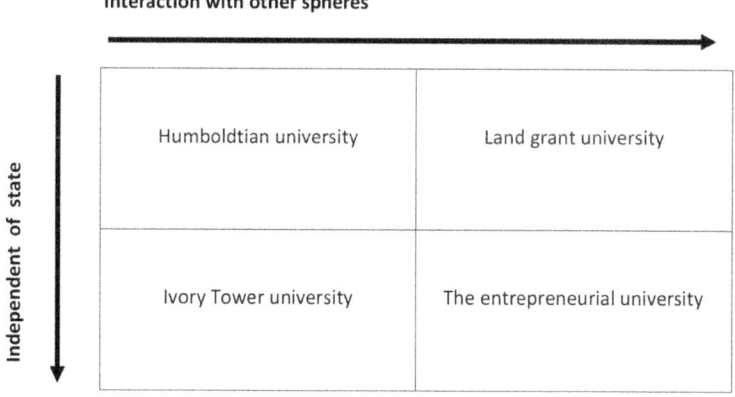

Source: Adapted from Etzkowitz, 2003, p. 318.

*Figure 2.1   Analytic approach to the second academic revolution*

Overall, this commonly acknowledged historiography of the university sets the life course of the university as a three-stage process that is punctuated by two academic revolutions. Most importantly, each "stage" or era is characterized by the addition of a new area of focus to the academic mission – teaching, research, and commercialization – with each of the three missions, although born from the social context of a specific era, added onto its preceding mission. As many historians of the university have acknowledged, while a specific organizing logic is dominant in each era in the history of the university, practices carrying this logic commonly began to appear before the watershed event we now conceptualize as an academic revolution. In this spirit, Etzkowitz (2003) explained how "academia–industry relations have long been present" (p. 318) prior to the second academic revolution that brought about the entrepreneurial university, with academic pharmaceutical sciences and chemistry being related to the development of German pharmaceutical and dye-stuff industries, respectively. Likewise, Marie-Laure Djelic (2012, p. 99) graphically illustrated that the roles and missions of universities continued on from one era to another, between two proximate regimes: practices associated with the "serving science" mission and role, as well as "serving state and nation", are evident in the era preceding the first academic revolution, even if this is the dominant theme of the Westphalian university.

The analytic tone of this historiography of universities' millennium-long life assumes that eras and revolutions indicate changes in the functional relevancy of the university and of academic knowledge to society. In this regard, the social so-called functions of the university are explained as evolving in response to civilizational changes (Kerr, 1963/2001), funding pressures (Press and Washburn, 2000), or capitalist demands (Deem, 2001; Slaughter and Rhoades, 2004). Also, alongside academic knowledge that has developed to fit the evolving social role of academia, therefore changing from "Mode 1" (which clearly differentiates between academic knowledge for its own sake, namely "basic science", and production-relevant knowledge, namely "applied science") to "Mode 2" (which blurs such distinction between basic and applied research due to the close cooperation between universities and industrial firms; Gibbons et al., 1994; Nowotny et al., 2001).

Interestingly, of the university's three missions, only this third mission is criticized as a corruption of academia and science. Whereas teaching and research are accepted as essential elements in the definition of the university, commercialization and entrepreneurism are frequently attacked as evidence for the penetration of market logics into the university. On this note, analyses of the commercialization of university knowledge drive the labelling of the contemporary university as "market university" (Berman, 2011) and "enterprise university" (Marginson and Considine, 2000). Most critical of the studies on marketization or managerialism of the university is the literature on "academic capitalism" (see the most comprehensive statement in Slaughter and Rhoades, 2004; also, for global and comparative perspective, see various chapters in Currie and Newson, 1998). From this critical perspective, Burton Clark's (1998, 2004) analysis of the university as diversifying its income sources – so as not to be beholden to politicians and bureaucrats for budgeting higher education and academic research – is further critiqued by Sheila Slaughter, Gary Rhoades, and Larry Leslie as universities being beholden to profit-maximizing corporations (see also Press and Washburn, 2000). Moreover, the university that Burton Clark (1998, 2004) described as an "entrepreneurial university" is critiqued by Clyde Barrow (2018) as a corporate university with academicians and entrepreneurial intellectuals. Describing this change in funding sources and economic logics among American public research universities, Diane Rhoten and Woody Powell (2010) aptly titled their paper "From Land Grant to Federal Grant to Patent Grant Institutions". They describe the transition of American universities from being publicly funded to profit-making organizations. As a result, the once-obvious distinction between universities that regard themselves as "cathedrals of learning" and their current operations as corporate "cathedrals of earning" (Engwall, 2008, p. 9; see also, Serrano-Velarde and Krücken, 2012; Willmott, 1995) is now blurred. The university is presently dominated by ideas and strategies that, until recently, have been antithetical to the spirit of academia (Drori, 2016). Importantly, this change seeps from the university's management to its members; for example, Della Porta et al. (2020) show that whereas student protests of the 1960s "emphasized the emergence of cultural and post-materialistic grievances" (p. 6), student protests of the 2000s respond to the marketization and commodification of higher education and contest primarily tuition fees. Slaughter (2001) summarized this critique by pointing out the threats that the dependence on for-profit partners and the incorporation of market logics pose to academic science.

In her analysis of Novartis' research partnership with universities, she wrote the following:

> (1) creation of new circuits of knowledge that link the academy to the economy; (2) development of an administrative preference for science and technology able to generate external revenues, which undermines academic autonomy and credibility and threatens institutional potential for critique; and (3) weakening of faculty self-governance, which underpins the exercise of academic freedom on campus. (p. 250)

With such a critique, "[t]he theory of academic capitalism moves beyond thinking of the student as consumer to considering the institution as marketer" (Slaughter and Rhoades, 2004, p. 1). In this regard, it is made clear that the debate over university partnership with the for-profit sector – whether it is an expansive entrepreneurial university or a university crippled by capitalism – is set on the basis of a sweeping agreement: the university of the late 20th century is heavily engaged with society, mostly with the economy and industry but also with government agencies and policymakers.

Still, rapid and global changes, which pose new challenges on the university's existing and traditional structures, practices and ethos, call on the present-day university to re-reassess its engagement with society and to adapt its structure and operations according to changing circumstances. While the notion of "mission drift" stirs negative connotations (of risks associated with unrestrained organizational changes or harmful "mission overload"), we argue that universities have a long and successful track record of sedimentation of their academic missions, with one mission added to another, rather than replacing it. With that, we argue, universities are and should continue reflecting upon societal changes and adjust their relationship with society accordingly. In the following section, we consider those societal changes that challenge whether the current university model is appropriate and sustainable.

## THIRD ACADEMIC REVOLUTION? CURRENT CHALLENGES TO THE UNIVERSITY ETHOS

These days, pressures are mounting on the institution of the university from various directions. Correspondingly, numerous analyses and commentaries urge universities to go *beyond* the third mission[3] and to reorient their mission towards engagement and impact.[4] And while the historic transformations are most dramatic for western universities, in the "old world" that is home to the age-old established universities (see, Kipping et al., 2004; Krücken et al., 2007, 2009; Mazza et al., 2008; Musselin, 2013), the challenges mounting on universities are felt and discussed worldwide. Do these pressures amount to a contemporary existential crisis of the institution? Might these pressures amass into a third academic revolution occurring in these times? Before considering the possibility that contemporary universities may be facing a transition into a fourth phase of the institution's millennium-long history, defined by a fourth academic mission, the following section describes the many challenges brought before universities these days.

First and probably foremost, universities are challenged by the rapidly expanding knowledge economy. With knowledge becoming the prized commodity of world trade, organizations of various sorts are driven to prosper through innovation and, with it, knowledge creation. Whereas universities once held the monopoly over knowledge creation – and surely the creation of basic science – for several decades, for-profit corporations have actively taken part in the generation of knowledge that does not have immediate or direct applications in production and commerce. For example, Bell Labs, which has its origins in Alexander Graham Bell's laboratory of the 1880s, investigated all sorts of physical and chemical properties of matter, which subsequently resulted in revolutionary technologies such as the synchronous-sound motion picture and the Unix operating system, and it earned the company's researchers eight Nobel Prizes and three Turing Awards.

A contemporary parallel can be seen at Google AI, whose enterprise combines basic and applied science practices so as to provoke the traditional disciplines of biology, chemistry, medicine, cognition, and environmental sciences, while also seeking solutions for Google-specific technologies such as Google Translate and e-mail. Also, for-profit consultancies operate research centres that produce reports and publications that rival academic publications; one is challenged to differentiate the economic analyses published in McKinsey & Co.'s *McKinsey Quarterly Magazine* from those of *Harvard Business Review*. Finally, think tanks and non-profit research centres – whether of governmental agencies, international organizations, or interest groups – also became sources for research-based knowledge. From the RAND corporation to the research divisions of intergovernmental and civil society organizations, such as the Organisation for Economic Co-operation and Development (OECD), the World Bank, Transparency International, and Human Rights Watch, non-profit bodies are equally committed to using cutting-edge scientific methods to compile data and produce new knowledge. In these ways, a variety of organizations are currently encroaching on the academic mission of research and the task of knowledge creation for their own sakes, which for centuries have been the domain of the university's privilege of concentrating on basic science.

Second, universities are also challenged by technological advances that are usurping, or at least dramatically altering, the ways universities are set to teach, research, and commercialize. Most obviously, the digital revolution allows for remote learning in ways that are profoundly different from the pen-paper-envelope-and-stamp version that was customary in, for example, open universities. Online studies, massive open online courses (known as MOOCs), and reverse classrooms are just a few of the platforms and related pedagogies that are made available during this WWW era. The currently raging coronavirus pandemic drove universities to hastily move their teaching, research, and operations onto such online platforms. These technological means surely changed the reaches of academic teaching by allowing academic study at remote regions of the world, even if evidence is accumulating to show that inequality in higher education and science learning persists (Drori, 2005). Importantly, while experimentation with such teaching sprang from elite universities, with Stanford University being the birthplace of Udacity and Coursera and a Harvard and MIT partnership creating edX, cutting-edge research and better-quality education are proven now to be the product of interpersonal learning and well-equipped facilities that are obviously not deliverable online. Nevertheless, universities worldwide are forcefully driven to change in order to adapt to the new technologies of information and communications and to the new forms of study that are relevant for the incoming students from the X and Y generations. Indeed, several high-tech changes have already been widely accepted by university teaching and research: for example, university courses are run through Moodle, students seek academic publications not by walking into the library but through online searches, and faculty are required to distinguish between and explain the marked difference between peer-reviewed publications and Wiki entries. These changes go beyond the means of technology; thus, they challenge the academic criteria for knowledge, its validity, and its acquisition.

Third, universities are challenged by labour market demands to justify the relevance of higher education for employable skills, job market placement, and work processes. Universities have only recently been included in debates surrounding the matching of education with labour market needs: whereas primary and secondary education debates have been raging for decades over the content of appropriate education (e.g., vocational and skills-based or scholastic and general), universities are currently measured by job placement of their graduates or by the reputation they have with employers. Graduate employability is refuted by academics as a relevant standard for universities: it is claimed that university education and research are all about erudition rather than knowhow, and therefore higher education is a marker of elite habitus rather than utility. Still, many proclaim the futility of academic education, especially in the humanities and basic science disciplines and for the growing masses of young people who are entering universities as part of the worldwide expansion of higher education. Most loudly, Peter Thiel, the famed German-American high-tech entrepreneur and founder of PayPal, awards a generous fellowship to, as its tag line states, "young people who want to build new things instead of sitting in a classroom".[5] Such calls drive universities to adapt: for instance, many traditional disciplines in universities give academic credit for internships in hopes of demonstrating the link between in-class experiences and on-the-job competencies. Still, even if they symbolically differentiate between faculties (for disciplinary sciences) and schools (for professional sciences), universities affirm that an academic education sets the basis for critical integrated thinking and thus provides valuable resource for the fast-changing and knowledge-based society of the 21st century; "We need philosophers, not only computer scientists" is the slogan universities use in recruiting students with start-up ambitions to enrol in the humanities. These make clear that the academic ethos still distances universities from labour market pressures.

Fourth, universities are increasingly strained under political pressures to adjust to political or public sentiments. This is a part of the centuries-old struggle of universities to maintain their professional autonomy and operational independence. Nevertheless, the general identification of the university as progressive and liberal is on many occasions at odds with the official ideological stance on social matters. Therefore, while opinion polls repeatedly confirm the public's trust in, and wide support for, universities, politicians are increasingly suspicious of academics and scorn their critique. Further political and more direct pressure is mounting on universities through funding: in regard to public universities in particular, which are by definition sponsored by politicians through state budgeting decisions, policies of privatization, accountability, and regulation often also envelop political censorship of academic expression. This type of political pressure formats the university as a "post-public" institution, which has been re-regulated and corporatized (e.g., Marginson, 2007). In addition, indirectly and thus more insidiously, change to political ideology in some countries drives many academics to emigrate: political–ideological battles in today's Turkey, as in Soviet countries during the Cold War, fuel a "voluntary brain drain" that results in changes to local academia.

Fifth, sociocultural changes add pressure to today's universities, even if not through the voting booth. The public's wide support for higher education and research does not inhibit the public's resentment of academia as elitist and aloof. This sentiment creates inherent tension within universities. For example, one such dissonant dilemma in universities emerges in language. Recognizing science as translocal and excellence as universal, today's universities are driven to internationalize – that is, to publish in the best academic journals worldwide, to compete for the most competitive and world-renowned research grants, and to recruit the best faculty and students internationally. However, for universities in countries where English is not the first language, such efforts to internationalize require the transition of academic teaching and writing from the native language to English, which is accepted as "globalese" or modern lingua franca. As many academics argue, in such countries, especially those in the humanities and social sciences, this transition stunts the study of their own society and inhibits local scholarly and intellectual development. This, they argue, is at the root of the local public's perception of the university as being divorced from local society and operating from a culturally estranged ivory tower. More acutely, these days the public's distrust of public institutions and elected officials, as well as the striking phenomenon of fake news, reflect on the public's image of the university: as described by Geschwind et al. (2019, p. 7), it is fuelling the global wave of "post-truth, anti-elite and anti-expert knowledge regimes … challenging traditional conceptions of what counts as legitimate knowledge, putting additional pressures on universities to proactively respond in accordance to their enlightenment and democratically inspired ideals". Under such global cultural transformations, universities are pressured to adapt to this public perception, and, as we further develop throughout this book, here lies the most important impetus for universities to develop a model of social commitment and leadership.

Last, universities nowadays come under pressure from administrative and governance reforms, which impose operational demands that come to detract from the primary academic operations at universities. These administrative and governance reforms bring new public management (NPM) to universities: starting in the UK in the 1980s and rapidly spreading to academic systems worldwide, university administration and governance were rearranged to meet performance standards, streamline administrative operations, establish HR management, and introduce service-oriented culture (see Bleiklie et al., 2011; Christensen, 2011). Importantly, although NPM discourse highlights academic autonomy alongside administrative prudence, NPM-driven reforms in universities change university practices and culture. By imposing performance criteria, these NPM reforms change the orientation of teaching and research (see Enders et al., 2015), alter the form and extent of faculty involvement in the leadership of universities (see Gerber, 2014; Huisman et al., 2006; Kaufman-Osborn, 2017; Lamont, 2009), and transform the ethos of universities (see Kallio et al., 2016). Such changes are magnified by the global dimensions of university governance, namely its transnational and multilevel form (Amaral et al., 2013; Altbach, 2016; Austin and Jones, 2015; Frost et al., 2016) and the involvement of intermediary organizations (Sahlin et al., 2015). These administrative and governance demands come alongside commercialization and marketization pressures; each in their unique way challenge contemporary universities to adapt to a rapidly changing global social context.

Overall, the institution of the university – in spite of its evolution to be guided by the three missions of teaching, research, and commercialization – is challenged by the knowledge economy. The knowledge economy offers alternative sites for knowledge production: (1) using technologies that enable alternative modes of learning and teaching, (2) through the labour market that demands specific skills rather than general erudition, (3) by political sentiments that promote the privatization of public sector commitments and thus curb public funding for higher education and academic research, (4) by sociocultural winds that currently blow in the direction of non-, if not anti-, universalist and humanist directions, and (5) by NPM reforms of university administration and governance that rearrange traditional academic roles and tasks. Combined, these diverse challenges redefine the meaning of knowledge – see Nowotny et al.'s (2001) Mode I and Mode II – and call into question the social role of universities. These changes also drive many observers of the university to question the tripartite distinction of the missions of universities (e.g., Laredo, 2007; Trencher et al., 2014) in spite of its convenient match with the historical evolution of the university's form. The societal changes and challenges to the university raise the following question: are universities still beacons for humanity's quest for knowledge and for progress through knowledge or are they conservative sites for the old elite and a socially aloof ivory tower? Whatever the position on such matters may be, the ethos of knowledge and science as the foundation for civilization has not been shaken. Therefore, whatever that position may be, universities are currently contemplating their relevance to and engagement with society and wrestling their ability to respond to world society's grand challenges. This is the basis for a discussion of the possibility of a fourth academic mission.

## THE FOURTH ACADEMIC MISSION: AN ONTOLOGICAL TURN TOWARDS "COMMITMENT AND LEADERSHIP"

Most historians of the university delineate eras and revolutions by the prime mission or task of the university – teaching, research, and commercial engagement. While confirming the same periodization, Djelic (2012) reorganized this history around the object of university service: service of God and the church, service of state and nation, service of society and humanity, and service of the market. By proposing academic commitment and leadership (ACL), we challenge Djelic on the formulation of the "postmodern" university of the late 20th century. Whereas Djelic described the 20th-century university as organized towards the service of society and humanity, we wish to highlight that, until recently, the university mission of social engagement was narrowly defined by involvement in the market. Only lately, with much still ahead of us, has the university been engaging with society in spheres that are not strictly commercialized and marketized. As described earlier, the entrepreneurial or market university, or academic capitalism, was primarily engaged with production and commerce. In this way, Djelic's (2012) labelling of the "entrepreneurial university" as one in service of society and humanity is rather misleading and overstates the university's commitment to developmentalism as distinct from its service for the market (pp. 101–103). As an alternative, the focus we propose in this book for the fourth academic mission underscores that, owing to the recent criticism of universities (see in following section), universities are currently broadening their academic mission to include the commitment and leadership of social causes beyond economic or technological development. Rather than expecting that development would "trickle down" to affect societal welfare, the fourth version of academic mission sets an academic commitment to advancing the public good and social agenda and to fostering leadership of social change as a distinct and integral goal of academic education.

How is the fourth mission distinct from the third mission of entrepreneurial and knowledge commercialization engagement? As noted above, the prime difference is that the entrepreneurial university model focused such engagement on relations with the market, industry, and public-governmental sector. This is most clearly captured in the idealization of the triple helix model of university–industry–government connections as the engine for regional and knowledge-based development; this valorization has given power to the global diffusion of this model, propelling this particular definition of the university's engagement with society. The fourth mission agenda, on the other hand, broadens the scope of a social agenda that is to be transformed through academic action. As we detail in the following chapters (particularly Table 4.1), the ACL university lays claim to a variety of social agendas: from just labour practices in the university and beyond, to teaching beyond the gates of the university and inclusionary policies of integrating otherwise marginalized groups into higher education, to the academic impact on policymaking, to the leadership of civic society action, and more.

One can also distinguish between the third and fourth academic missions with the schematic differentiation between university "push" and "pull" factors. If the third mission positions the university as "pulled" into engagement with society because of industrial demands or societal needs, the fourth mission defines the university as "pushing" new ideas/ technologies or services to society. In this regard, the third academic mission brings university inventions and innovations to the public, primarily focusing on the developmental needs of society, and the ACL model describes a different emergence trajectory, generally seeing the university as *responsible* for the public good and engaged with public action; see, for example, the various discussions in Holmwood (2011). The fourth mission is, therefore, propelled by the institutionalization of CSR norms in the for-profit sector and the trickling of such norms to public sector organizations. This normative shift worldwide towards CSR exerts pressure on the university to reconsider and reconceptualize, as well as institutionalize into actionable practices, the leadership and responsibility role of universities with regards to society.

The ideological alertness and expressed commitment by many academicians for ACL (as a general theme, not yet categorized or classified in any way) are also related to some powerful evidence from the academic research that shows the value of civic involvement and enhanced social capital. For instance, the seminal work by Putnam (2000) offered the compelling argument that civic engagement and close and cohesive networks among social groups are characterized in various civil-based parameters such as high level of voter turnout, newspaper readership, membership in choral societies, and football clubs (found in the early study in Italy; see Leonardi et al., 2001). These factors of social and civil cohesion were found to be associated with the important outcome of civic measures such as better schools, faster growing economic development, lower crime, and more effective government.

By the same token, we can expect that increased actions of ACL in society could be associated with some other important outcomes. These include, for example, a stronger and more challenging elementary and high school education system or better healthcare practices and services for privileged groups with health needs. Additional outcomes include higher levels of exposure to advanced research and its applied aspects that could positively affect society and promote a higher level of awareness on critical civil and social processes that take place in shaping one's personal development. These changes on the individual level could lead to a significant change at the regional or national level if universities became more engaged in general societal needs.

These new trends of ACL are only emerging and are not yet sufficiently diffused among universities in different countries. Moreover, as far as we have learned through discussions with colleagues, there are no leading models of ACL that have yet emerged as prescriptions for accepted practices. At this point, there are only initial understandings of the importance to act on this front; in this sense, this book combines descriptive components with normative and prescriptive components. We aim to describe the reorientation of universities towards a fourth mission of social engagement, which we define as the ACL model of the university's societal engagement. We also aim to promote this vision of university engagement as an appropriate model for the 21st-century university. On the descriptive level, we draw on many examples of universities broadening their academic mission and sociological and organizational theories; also, we pose a critical perspective, considering the prices or constraints that ACL imposes on the changing institution of the university.

A university is a place where the universality of the human spirit manifests itself. ... I should like to express the hope that our university will always be free of the evil [of chauvinism, blind intolerance and nationalism], that teachers and students will always preserve the consciousness that they serve their people best when they maintain its union with humanity and with the highest human values. (Albert Einstein, "The Mission of our University", *New Palestine*, 27 March 1925, 13: 294)

## NOTES

1. For a discussion of the university from such a legalistic perspective, see, for example, Duryea and Williams (2013), Lane and Kinser (2011), Palfreyman and Tapper (2014), and the textbook by Kaplin and Lee (2011).
2. For discussion of university from such an economic perspective, see, for example, Palfreyman and Tapper (2014), Raines and Leathers (2003), and West (1995/2018).
3. See, for example, Bacevic (2017), Geschwind et al. (2019), Guenther (2019), Kretz and Sá (2013), Nedeva (2007), and Pinheiro et al. (2015).
4. See, primarily, Bok (2009), but also Eyal and Bucholz (2010), Thune et al. (2016), and Watermeyer (2012a, 2012b).
5. https://thielfellowship.org, accessed 7 August 2018.

# 3. The shaping of contemporary models for the university's public role: from CSR to ACL

In Chapter 2, we claimed that the institution of a university has a long record of social engagement with and responsibility towards society. Over the millennium-long university–society relations, this commitment has changed periodically. Now comes the time for re-adjustment for the 21st century. In this chapter, we aim to review the concept and practices associated with corporate social responsibility (CSR) and show how the models share similarities and differences from our conception of academic commitment and leadership (ACL). In an effort to establish the conceptual grounds for ACL, this chapter builds on the wide recognition of CSR, which frames any discussion about the social impact of individuals and organizations from the past few decades. Indeed, organization theory and research in the last decade are rich with articles and books on CSR.[1] However, the applicability of this stream of research to issues of academic leadership and commitment to social import is neither direct nor obvious. Therefore, our aim is to explore the impact of CSR's legacy on any new models for social impact, whether CSR elements can be translated to a theoretical model of ACL, and whether these elements can reflect on the domain of universities and their changing missions in society.

We return to the definition of ACL that we introduced in Chapter 2. Our definition of ACL is based on orienting *academic commitment and leadership* towards the advancement of public goods and social issues. Our definition builds on three main elements:

1. Advance the public good and social issues – the focus of this fourth mission is to contribute to important social issues and, as a result, advance public goods.
2. Foster academic leadership of social change – we believe that this mission is driven by academicians and scientists and thus is characterized as a "bottom-up" process of responsibility and action

towards the goals mentioned in the first element. This mission is not independent of the other first three missions of the university (e.g., teaching, research, and technology transfer) but is interwoven into academic socialization of these three missions.
3. Institutionalize practices that encourage ACL and socialize new entrants to the university into a normative culture.

Together, the three defining elements weave together a description of the goal (public good), the actors (academicians), and the form (socialization into normative culture of ACL). In reference to these three elements, we further clarify that we do not refer to mere volunteering by academicians but to issues of personal involvement and commitment. With regards to the organizational process involved in ACL, we do not refer to top-down organizational processes that are used in CSR managerial practices. Finally, we do not necessarily refer to the public good actions that are derived from, or directly linked with, the academic task of teaching, research, or commercialization. ACL can refer to actions taken by academicians or scientists with regards to topics they feel close to and that are generally related to their area of commitment and leadership.

Patterns of change and adaptation within organizations can operate along two main epistemologies. On the one hand, there are evolutionary processes that lead to changes in the qualities, structures, goals, or practices of any organizational form. These changes result from adaptation needs of the specific organizational form due to environmental or process-based changes. On the other hand, organizations are exposed to external pressures coming from various stakeholders in their environments (DiMaggio and Powell, 1983). These changes may result from a need to adapt to accepted practices or norms that are taken by other organizational forms that coexist within the operational environment. We distinguish between these two adaptation processes. One is an evolutionary process, whereas the other is a translation process.

This chapter deals with the "translation" process from CSR to ACL. It is based on a cross-sectional analytical framework where organizational forms can borrow some elements adopted by other organizational forms coexisting in their operational environment. They can adapt the same practices as a whole or choose a few of these practices, they can initiate some practices and change the way they operate them, or they can take some practices on one organizational level and adapt them on another level. All of these modes of translation of practices can take place. The main question here is, if ACL represents a cultural shift for the missions of the university, what CSR practices can be translated and under what conditions will they match the other organizational form of the university? The challenge here is to offer a critical focus on the concept of translation (Phillips et al., 2000) of rules and resources from one field to another. Following the translation from CSR to ACL, it is important to focus on the specific context in which it takes place and the specific characteristics associated with this context.

In this context, a comment on clarification is needed. Using the term "translation", we do not aim to indicate that universities are necessarily practicing an urge to adapt CSR practices. Our interest is conceptual and analytical as we aim to question the degree to which CSR goals and practices are relevant to universities and the practices of ACL.

## TRANSLATION FROM CORPORATE SOCIAL RESPONSIBILITY (CSR)

This chapter aims to introduce the main literature on CSR and examine its relevant features to ACL. Seeing the expanse and dominance of CSR literature over the past seven or so decades (Carroll, 1999), CSR has come to influence all discussions of social engagement and impact of organizations of all sorts – including the university, which is increasingly described as "an organization" (Krücken and Meier, 2006) and is increasingly managerialized and corporatized (e.g., Deem and Brehony, 2005; Donoghue, 2018; Drori, 2016; Engwall, 2008). And yet, because CSR emerged from, and is thus is imprinted by, the field of for-profit organizations, the question of translation of CSR to ACL requires a detailed review of the commonalities and differences between the fields. We start by reviewing the most dominant and highly cited literature on CSR to establish the initial grounds for examining the commonalities/differences.

**The Legacy of CSR**

CSR is an organizational trend or practice that takes place within for-profit organizations, and it has appeared in the organizational literature for at least seven decades (Carroll, 1999). The main thrust of this organizational trend and practice is that, aside from their main goal (e.g., for-profit activities), for-profit organizations must be engaged in socially oriented activities.

Even after many years of research on the topic, defining CSR is a challenging task (Malik, 2015). Some researchers have considered CSR to be a function of a firm's behaviour towards its stakeholders, including customers, suppliers, regulators, employees, investors, and communities (Campbell, 2007). Other researchers have defined CSR as a company's flexible multi-range activities, including social, political, environmental, economic, and ethical actions (Devinney, 2009). In an historical review of the concept of CSR, Archie Carroll (1999) listed numerous definitions going back as far as 1950. He concluded his detailed review by stating, "The CSR concept will remain as an essential part of business language and practice, because it is a vital underpinning to many of the other theories and is continually consistent with what the public expects of the business community today" (Carroll, 1999, p. 292).

Carroll (1999) also added that as the theory of CSR is developed and further research is conducted, scholars may continue to revise existing definitions of CSR or offer new definitions. However, it is difficult to imagine that these new concepts could develop apart from the groundwork that has been established over the past half century. It is highly likely that we will see a new organizational culture in which the concept of business responsibilities to the stakeholder society becomes an issue that is taken for granted. He concluded that "In this context, it appears that the CSR concept has a bright future because at its core, it addresses and captures the most important concerns of the public regarding business and society relationships" (Carroll, 1999, p. 292).

In this chapter, we analyse some of the central insights from the recent literature on CSR. In addition, based on a critical review of the central themes of CSR, the chapter will explore the translation potential of CSR for ACL and whether there are parallels or distinct foundations for both concepts.

In a recent reference to CSR, Carroll (2016) claimed that the structure of a pyramid is a geometric design because it is simple and intuitive. In this hierarchical triangular structure, the economic responsibility of firms is at the base due to its basic requirement for a sustainable business. Above the economic responsibility, this structure also depicts the societal expectation that a business will obey the law and regulations because these are society's basic "ground rules" for businesses that operate in civil society. Next, ethical norms are important for the operation of businesses, and they should express the obligation to do "what is right, just, and fair and to avoid or minimize harm to all the stakeholders with whom it interacts" (p. 410). At the top of the pyramid is the expectation that businesses will be good corporate citizens in the sense of acting in a philanthropic manner and give back to the community in various ways

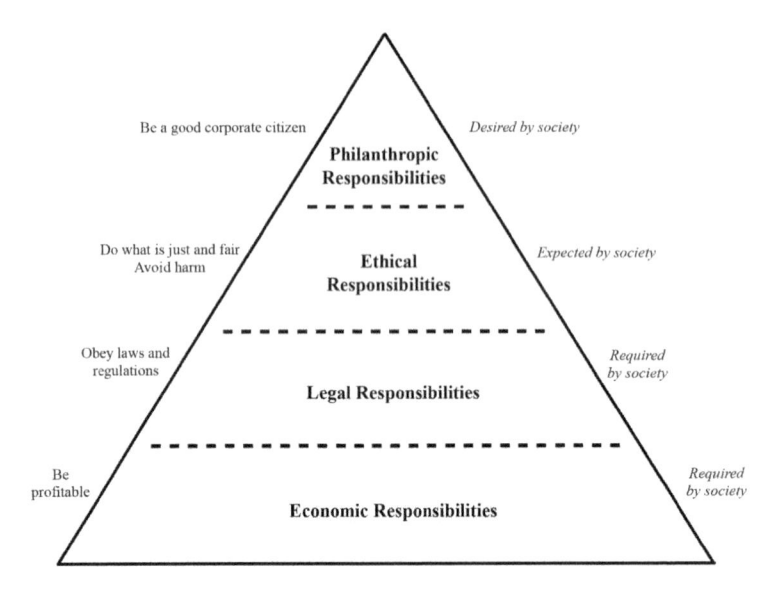

*Figure 3.1    Carroll's pyramid model of CSR (2016, p. 5)*

and modes. We use this model (Figure 3.1) to illustrate the main characterization of CSR as a model that has influenced the conception of ACL. However, this CSR does not have a single format and is not free from criticism. To further this discussion on ACL, we would like to review a few CSR framings and criticisms of these models.

## Models of CSR

In a critical review of the CSR literature, O'Riordan and Fairbrass (2008) claimed that CSR is not a new concept. It remains an elusive concept treated in various ways by academicians, industry people, businesses, and stakeholders. Due to the variety of definitions and perceptions, numerous firms associate the concept of CSR with various practices (Crane and Matten, 2004). The concept was first introduced in the 1950s (Carroll, 1999), and after so many years, it seems that there is still little agreement about what the term means and how it can be translated into relevant organizational practices or implemented in organizations (O'Riordan and Fairbrass, 2008).

It can be argued that the wide spectrum of definitions offered for the term CSR appears to arise from the many different perceptions held by individuals in relation to the question of business responsibility and obligation. In the same manner, while also aiming to establish an operational definition, Factor et al. (2013) noted that:

> Uses and definitions of CSR have evolved over time . . . and there remains no consensus on its definition today. While we leave to others a more detailed discussion of this debate, we note that, despite this lack of consensus . . . a general theme at the core of CSR includes the normative responsibility of organizations toward the welfare of others in the community and society in general. (p. 144)

Two questions are evident here: (1) "Why do we observe such a large range of perceptions of CSR?"; and (2) "Is there, among all the different perceptions and approaches, a 'core-skeleton' concept of CSR that can be examined and developed systematically?" The first question is answered by Factor et al. (2013). They suggested that the issue can be clarified through the institutional theory that discusses various institutional pressures by various stakeholders. As they claimed,

> Two recent theoretical papers, by Aguilera et al. (2007) and Campbell (2007), advance our thinking about why differences in CSR beliefs may exist. Both use an institutional framework that urges scholars to take note of the strong, but varied, legal and quasi-legal pressures from governments, nongovernmental organizations and other stakeholders to encourage corporations to engage in CSR within their own countries. In addition, multinational corporations face intensified pressures across national borders to do likewise. (Factor et al., 2013, p. 144)

As to the second issue of a "core-skeleton" component of CSR, this is a complex issue, and it is difficult to detect the main components that are accepted as valid constructs or reliable measures of CSR. This is an even greater challenge since we know from the literature that there is a great gap between rhetoric and reality concerning CSR policy and practice (O'Riordan and Fairbrass, 2008). This means that even if we find a common agreement on the components of the definition of CSR, their transformation into practices is not a clear or transparent process.

In terms of how to resolve this ambiguity concerning the CSR concept, it may be useful to use formal definitions offered by prominent formal organizations. Here are several examples for such definitions. The World Business Council on Sustainable Development (WBCSD, 2013) suggested the following: "Corporate Social Responsibility is the continuing commitment by business to contribute to economic development while improving the quality of life of the workforce and their families as well as of the community and society at large."[2] In 2012, the European Commission defined CSR as "the responsibility of enterprises for their impacts on society". To fully meet their social responsibility, enterprises "should have in place a process to integrate social, environmental, ethical human rights and consumer concerns into their business operations and core strategy in close collaboration with their stakeholders".[3] Also, the Foreign Affairs and International Trade Canada defined CSR in 2013 as:

> The voluntary activities undertaken by a company to operate in an economic, social and environmentally sustainable manner. Canadian companies recognize the value of incorporating CSR practices into their operations abroad. Operating responsibly also plays an important role in promoting Canadian values internationally and contributes to the sustainable development of communities.[4]

These three definitions of CSR, although reflecting the conception of three randomly selected and prominent organizations, share several components for CSR. They all offer a positive tone and expectation that CSR activities will have a positive impact on society. However, there are differences between these definitions. The first definition focuses on "commitment", the second on "responsibility", and the third on "voluntary activities" as the core concept that applies to the motivation of the "focal action taker", meaning the social unit that is expected to act as socially responsible. Also, if we want to learn about the identity of the focal action taker, we see again a range of options (i.e., the "business", the "enterprise", and the "company") in the three definitions, respectively.

What are these businesses, enterprises, or companies expected to do in order to act with social responsibility? In the first definition, they have to "contribute to economic development while improving the quality of life of the workforce and their families as well as of the community and society at large" (Dahlsrud, 2008, p. 4). This means that they have to, on top of contributing to economic development, act both internally towards improving their workers' and their families' quality of life and externally for the community and society at large. Thus, they are responsible for everything around them. The second definition claims that they need to have in place a process to integrate social, environmental, and ethical human rights and consumer concerns into their business operations and core strategy in close collaboration with their stakeholders (Morsing and

Schultz, 2006). The meaning of the second definition is that they must establish a formal organizational procedure that will be responsible for carrying out the actions needed to be considered "socially responsible". Also, the third definition focuses on the ambiguous claim that they have to "operate in an economic, social and environmentally sustainable manner" (Cegarra-Navarro et al., 2016, p. 530). This operation is both within and outside of the country, focusing on the dissemination and diffusion of the country's values internationally.

Finally, we need to ask, who are the beneficiaries? Namely, who are those who will benefit from the socially responsible actions taken by the corporate entity? These potential beneficiaries also vary across the three definitions. Beneficiaries range from the workforces and their families, community, and society in the first definition to the stakeholders in the second definition. The third definition is ambiguous in this respect and seems to focus on the "sustainable international communities" wherever the country's companies operate.

In summing up this exercise, we have shown here a random sample of three definitions offered by large international business and trade organizations. All three definitions offer formal and seemingly operational definitions of CSR. However, it is difficult to find clear "core" elements or the skeleton offered by these three definitions, aside from the general message of "doing good" in one way or another. The message remains opaque and ambiguous, and thus open to interpretations and translations of the organizations operating, their managers and stakeholders associated with the organizational activities.

Whether this ambiguity is good or bad is a philosophical and operational question. For our purpose, it is sufficient to point out that there does not seem to be an agreement between various formal organizations in their reference to CSR and that this lack of definitional agreement does not prevent these organizations from operating in the context of the suggested definition.

In summary, the main claim and organizing principle of this section is that no matter what the definition of CSR is or what exact practices are materializing in any of the definitions, the important matter is that CSR dominates every discussion of social impact. Therefore, our framing question is, does CSR at all fit with universities, science, and ACL? In this regard, we are self-critical of the very issue of translation, and although we started with this concept in the first section, we are ready to change the tone here. We claim that CSR is a dominant concept in the context of for-profit organizations. However, our claim originates from an institutional approach to organizations and starts with the ambiguity of CSR and the evidence we cite for the lack of coherent definitions. This, coupled with the dominance of CSR over the field of social impact, gives it particular might and drives its adoption in universities. However, we argue that this adoption should be challenged and requires a more detailed inquiry. This is due to the incomparability of universities and academia. Universities have already adopted a third mission of technology transfer as a part of their social mission. The addition we introduce – of ACL – depicts a reorientation of universities towards their fourth mission.

### Stakeholders' Role in CSR and Stakeholders' Dialogues

It is apparent from the three definitions presented above that the related organizational stakeholders and their interrelations serve an important role in the process of developing CSR practices by firms. What are the "stakeholders" in this context? From the literature, we learned that the term "stakeholder(s)" has a broad-ranging scope. One way in which it has been defined is that all those individuals and groups have a "critical eye" on corporate actors and are thus important actors operating in the environment of the organization (Bomann-Larsen and Wiggen, 2004). Thus, stakeholders are defined and characterized by the main organizational missions or goals.

Such stakeholders can act in a formal or informal way, as individuals or as collectives, but it is clear that they are an important part of the organization's external environment. It is also clear that the stakeholders can have a positive or negative impact on the organization that is practicing CSR (Murray and Vogel, 1997). The main challenge for firms is the task involved in identifying the main stakeholders (e.g., to whom the firm is responsible, in what form the responsibility takes, and to what degree that responsibility extends; O'Riordan and Fairbrass, 2008).

After identifying the institutional environment of CSR and the main stakeholders to whom firms are, or ought to be, socially responsible, the question is how to establish working relations with these stakeholders. There are various means by which firms contact, establish, and engage in relations with their stakeholders, and these range from direct relations or exchanges to distant and formal acts of responsibility with no prior relations or exchanges with the group.

To fulfil the chosen CSR obligations, firms can engage directly or indirectly with their stakeholders. One form of engagement with stakeholders is labelled "stakeholder dialogue". Such a dialogue is advantaged by the fact that it can offer firms and their stakeholders an opportunity to identify and jointly discuss the issues that each side regards as the best practice for CSR. In the context of firms based on CSR, the dialogues are usually in relation to economic, social, and environmental matters (O'Riordan and Fairbrass, 2008).

If there is such a dialogue between firms and their stakeholders in relation to the chosen and application of the CSR practices, they can face various difficulties. Some of the difficulties have been listed by O'Riordan and Fairbrass (2008, p. 749) and include the following: (1) conflicting expectations – where the expectations of both sides do not align and are even conflicting; and (2) contextual complexities that are associated with differences between geographical regions or different cultures between the firm and the stakeholders or various stakeholders.

The conception and practice of CSR in organizations have become a dominant discourse. Such a domination results in additional challenges. For example, issues associated with the choice of the best practice include the challenge of identifying and agreeing on what should be considered the best practice for the CSR dialogue and practice between the firm and stakeholders. Since there are various practices associated with firm–stakeholder dialogues and they also entail normative issues resulting from values, there are many potential complexities associated with the selection and retention of the best practice.

**Analytical Frameworks of CSR**

The dialogue about stakeholders in the literature is central to the rhetoric of CSR. This is due to the fact that if CSR is defined by the way organizations approach their stakeholders, it is important to specify the relevant stakeholders in the context of CSR organizational operation. For the purpose of focusing on a concrete analytical framework of stakeholder dialogue, we have chosen the one proposed by Aguinis and Glavas (2012). At this stage, mainly due to the very ambiguous and diverse definitions and approaches from the literature, a clear model of CSR, from which we can depart in order to examine the possible translation to ACL, is needed. The model presented below, adopted from Aguinis and Glavas (2012), illustrates the complexity of CSR and offers a good model of departure for examining the context of ACL.

## THEORIZING CSR AND CRITICAL ACCOUNTS FROM WITHIN THE PARADIGM

CSR came under criticism from many sides – some from "inside" the paradigm, by noting its misalignment with the corporate agenda (e.g., Claydon, 2011; Freeman and Velamuri, 2006; Jenkins, 2004), and most from "outside" the paradigm, because it is regarded as a "whitewashing" corporate strategy (e.g., Fleming and Jones, 2013; Pope and Wæraas, 2016). Joanna Tochman Campbell's (2007) critique of CSR is particularly poignant and analytic, and therefore we use it as a framework for our reference in analysing CSR and the subsequent proposal of ACL. Campbell claimed that most of the theoretically oriented research on CSR has focused on studying the connection between CSR and corporate financial performance. In addition, the emphasis in these studies was on determining the degree to which socially responsible corporate behaviour has an effect on the financial performance of for-profit organizations and not the other way around. Thus, the focus on maximizing the profit-making outcome for corporations leads to a cynical and critical approach to CSR. This is because, on the one hand, corporations will be acting irresponsibly if they do not do their utmost to increase their income. On the other hand, developing CSR organizational practices that are based only on financial motivations is a cynical act, since such practices assume commitment to the chosen activities that should not be monitored or calculated by loss or profit accounting.

Therefore, we agree that the theoretical approach to CSR should move from economic profit-making motivations to other theoretical approaches that focus on the behaviour of and choices made by organizations, and this is especially true when the focus is on ACL issues. In general, theories that do not focus on pure economic calculations and that study CSR can be classified into two streams of research: political economy and institutional theory (Campbell, 2007). Comparative political economy in political science argues that competitive conditions create the opportunities and incentives for firms to benefit from the "free ride" on the collective goods. These lead to many examples of irresponsible activities, and, in fact, the question needs to be, given the incentives to maximize profits and act opportunistically, what are the conditions that lead corporations to act with social responsibility?

Institutional analysis seeks to understand the role of institutions beyond the economic markets and assumes that the institutional forces in which corporations operate are the platform on which corporations decide how to treat their stakeholders, such as employees, customers, suppliers, and the communities within which they operate. Furthermore, Campbell (2007) offered propositions that predict the conditions under which corporations will choose to act with social responsibility. Since these propositions are also relevant to our theoretical understanding of ACL, we depict them here in a way that serves as a transition to understanding the possible institutional bases for ACL. We follow this with a description of four propositions offered by Campbell (2007), followed by their translation to the context of universities and ACL.

**Economic Conditions**

Campbell (2007) offers two propositions on the economic conditions in which corporations operate that have an impact on their tendency to act with social responsibility. First, when the corporation's financial performance is weak, or when the economic environment is experiencing problems, corporations are expected to be occupied by their financial survival and are less likely to act with social responsibility. Thus, Campbell's first proposition is that corporations will be less likely to act in socially responsible ways when they are experiencing relatively weak financial performance and when they operate in an environment where the possibility for near-term profitability is limited. The applicability of this first proposition to the context of universities and ACL seems straightforward. Under economic hardships, or when the environment in which universities operate experiences financial problems, the odds that universities will develop and maintain social responsibility practices are low. This is because, under such conditions, universities will not have the resources needed to develop social responsibility practices.

Campbell's (2007) second proposition pertains to competition, postulating that corporations will be less likely to act in socially responsible ways if there is either too much or too little competition. Applying this proposition to the academic context, universities also experience competition on the national and international levels, in their position in international rankings, for students who can pay high tuition fees, and over reputable and high-quality scientists and for research grants. The comparative context of the second proposition may result in having universities act with social responsibility when the competition with other institutions is too high or too little – when competition is high, social responsibility activities can add to the social position of the university and add to its reputation, and when it is low, universities can afford to act with social responsibility rather than focus only on competition with other universities.

**Institutional Conditions**

Campbell's (2007) third set of propositions pertains to the institutional conditions, postulating that the institutional conditions in which corporations operate have an impact on the degree to which they can develop and maintain social responsibility practices. Her third proposition is that corporations will be more likely to act in socially responsible ways if there are strong and well-enforced state regulations in place to ensure such behaviour, particularly if the process by which these regulations and enforcement capacities were developed was based on negotiation and consensus building among corporations, the government, and other relevant stakeholders. Such state regulations that go beyond the three main missions of universities – teaching, research, and technology transfer – are not commonly existing, and thus this proposition does not seem to have a direct relevance towards ACL practices. However, we started to observe some recent changes in this respect, as there is importance assigned to universities' ACL activities by funding agencies, ranking systems, and other stakeholders. While we list a series of ACL-guided strategies in Chapter 4, one notable example is the *Times Higher Education*'s ranking of universities according to four indexes of social impact and responsibility.

Campbell's (2007) fourth and last proposition on CSR that may have relevance to universities refers to the organizational field in which firms operate and the degree to which the various organizations in the field are generating the expectations for socially responsible activities offered by firms. The proposition claims the following: corporations will be more likely to act in socially responsible ways if there are private, independent organizations, including NGOs, social movement organizations, institutional investors, and the press, in their environment who monitor their behaviour and, when necessary, mobilize to change it.

The role of the normative environment described here as a change mobilizer is also applicable to universities. If the organizational field in which universities operate establishes expectations towards ACL and monitors the behaviour of universities so that they develop social responsibility practices, we will observe more ACL practices adopted by universities. These will match the expectations placed by the social organizations in their field. For example, if an NGO seeking better education for elementary school students is also seeking to assist students in their activities within schools every Friday, universities may cooperate with such expectations and reduce the class loads from students on Fridays and encourage their students to participate in these activities. Similarly, if a social movement calls for individuals' public attention to issues of poverty and they protest publicly, university professors and students (i.e., those who believe in these protesting activities) may be recruited to join them as university delegations.

Campbell's last proposition on CSR that is applicable to ACL refers to institutionalized dialogues with actors in the organizational field. Campbell claimed the following: corporations will be more likely to act in socially responsible ways if they are engaged in institutionalized dialogue with unions, employees, community groups, investors, and other stakeholders. In this context, once universities have established institutionalized dialogues with the various members of their community on issues related to the public, members of the workforces, and other stakeholders, it is expected that they will have higher odds for establishing social responsibility practices. Thus, continuous dialogue with the direct social environment leads to the establishment of socially responsible activities.

## CSR AND NEW PUBLIC MANAGEMENT IN UNIVERSITIES

We think that CSR has been adopted by universities as a component of their adoption of new public management (NPM) practices. As described by Ferlie et al. (2008), this public sector reform wave emerged in the UK during the 1980s but was adopted internationally in other countries including Sweden and New Zealand. This policy relied on strong performance measurement with monitoring and management systems rather than self-regulation with the addition of entrepreneurial managers instead of public sector professionals (see Bleiklie et al., 2011; Deem and Brehony, 2005; Schimank, 2005). NPM is reflected by the following: a stronger hierarchy at the top of the university, reduced interest-based representation of ex officio actors, more strategic business-like principles, and involvement from the society through the inclusion of external members of decision bodies (Ramirez and Christensen, 2013, p. 701). Importantly, some argue that NPM, and specifically the borrowing of the practice of CSR from for-profit companies (Jongbloed et al., 2008), are critical for securing the universities' much-needed public trust and public funding.

These changes lead to a paradox, by which the modern university reform has changed the university system from having low formal autonomy and high real autonomy to a situation of high formal autonomy and low actual autonomy. It may well be that the changing culture in universities to stronger management and weaker academic and professional elements, coupled with stronger environmental pressure, represents the decreasing real autonomy of universities (Christensen, 2011, p. 515).

In general, universities, much like for-profit firms, act under economic constraints and competition (especially with regards to NPM policies), which limits the availability to develop practices that are not directly related to making profit and survival. Only when these forces and constraints are not limiting a greater variety of activities, aside from the designated roles, will universities be able to develop a well-thought-out model of ACL and decide how to act for creating added value to their society.

At the same time, the institutional environment has a motivating and encouraging role. As it is for profit-oriented firms, when the institutional environment is placing expectations for socially responsible activities, and when there are established dialogues with stakeholders in the organizational field of the universities, the odds that universities will develop ACL practices increase and such activities will be well acknowledged and valued by the stakeholders and other social actors.

Due to the high dependency of corporations on the institutional environment that monitors their behaviours, Campbell (2007, pp. 958–962) argued that they will probably act in socially responsible ways. They are more likely to act with social responsibility when the environment in which they operate institutionalizes normative calls for such behaviour. A variety of practices have been adopted and implemented by universities as a part of their NPM administrative regime. Some are related to environmental preservation issues by universities (Ahmad, 2012; Sammalisto and Arvidsson, 2005), whereas others refer to economic, philanthropic, and environmental responsibility as well as employee wellness and legal responsibility (Asemah et al., 2013). These studies in particular reveal the variety of CSR practices implemented by universities as a part of their overall NPM administrative regime, with much of this variety resulting from global adaptations of the CSR regime to the local cultural and political contexts and to the higher education sector.

The literature has also provided references to the role of higher education, particularly management and business education, in socializing future managers into CSR. For example, Muijen (2004) claimed that the incorporation of CSR in universities cannot be successful only by means of compliance instructions but must also include a strategy that facilitates a transformation of the corporate culture level. Another study of business school curricula in Spain has examined the courses taught on CSR and found there are many standalone CSR courses (Setó-Pamies et al., 2011). Likewise, others (e.g., Ahmad, 2012; Muijen, 2004; Setó-Pamies et al., 2011) emphasized the socialization effect of higher education on future leaders, regarding such socialization as a component of the universities' CSR role.

This claim of adopting CSR strategies is also echoed in the work of Dahan and Senol (2012), who analysed the CSR-related activities adopted by Bilgi University in Istanbul. As a private university, Bilgi University was committed to CSR strategies for gaining a strong reputation and a competitive advantage. The study found that "in order for an institution to be successful in CSR strategy, CSR actions have to be internalized and must be supported by the management" (p. 95). Thus, this case study highlights the notion that universities conduct CSR because they are in the mode of managerialized organizations and because CSR is a component in the NPM regime that has been wholly adopted by some universities worldwide. We, however, claim that universities are not like all organizations for whom CSR is an appropriate format for engaging with society and its expectations. Rather, there is a need for universities to be a reformulation of CSR into ACL. Although universities, like other managed organizations, implement "standard" CSR practices, there are various areas of CSR that universities can pay attention to. As described by Asemah et al. (2013), universities already direct their CSR efforts at economic responsibility, philanthropic responsibility, environmental responsibility, employee wellness and health, employment of qualified lecturers, and legal responsibility. Our claim is that universities, because of their long history of varied engagements with society, should redirect their CSR "impulse" towards the format of ACL. We elaborate on this towards the end of this chapter.

## CSR FOR ACADEMIA? OR – WHY (OR WHY NOT) SHOULD UNIVERSITIES PRIORITIZE AN ACL MISSION? AN INSTITUTIONAL PERSPECTIVE

Recapping our claim, which is explained in Chapter 2, we argue that universities are considered to be organizational actors and a legitimized and vital part of society. As such, they are pressured to conform to the demands imposed on all other modern organizational actors and to meet the many challenges that societies face worldwide. Among these challenges is the call on universities to explore venues for full or partial independence from governmental support. As a result, higher education is facing major environmental changes. On the one hand, we observe a mass expansion of higher education, with new local and global academic organizations being established that generate increased competition among universities for students and funding (Marginson, 2006). In addition, there is a general decrease in state expenditure and support for universities (Cheslock and Gianneschi, 2008; Horta, 2009). Additional changes include the internationalization of academic programmes, the commercialization of universities, changes that are introduced by ICT development allowing for remote education, and the adaptation of new academic curricula to accommodate and capitalize on labour market requirements (Alzyoud and Bani-Hani, 2015).

The framing we suggest here is that CSR and universities are related though the definition of an "organization" (see Krücken and Meier, 2006; Ramirez and Christensen, 2013), as well as to its direct application to the missions of universities (see Kosmützky and Krücken, 2015). Our claim is that under the new challenges that universities are facing, they understand the need to redefine their social role. However, because the discourse of social impact is dominated by CSR, universities wrestle with the "C" dimension of CSR and thus lack a clear conception of what "SR" is for them. Thus, this book is dedicated to the proposition and development of an alternative concept – ACL – that originates within the operation missions of universities and adheres to the activities that are uniquely featured within universities.

It is apparent that these changes have and will continue to have an impact on the various important aspects of the university, such as the quality of education and the level of university autonomy, and on the level of academic freedom. These changes will probably have an impact on the changing missions of universities and their responsibilities towards society. The current general trend, in which universities are moving towards corporatization (see Donoghue, 2018; Tuchman, 2009), aligns with the existing social expectations for an organization to be an ethical and socially responsible corporate citizen. The question is whether the best approach for universities is to adapt to the corporate concept and norm of social responsibility.

As some argue, universities could achieve greater legitimacy, sustainability, and competitiveness by adding social responsibility actions to their missions (Alzyoud and Bani-Hani, 2015). However, we claim that it is important to be sensitive to the unique features of universities and their additional roles in society in order to consider an effective and non-cynical adaptation of norms of commitment and leadership, while also maintaining the important three initial missions that have been fulfilled by universities so far. The adaptation process in which universities can integrate the ACL mission into their activities should be considered through a theoretical paradigm rather than a corporate strategy approach, as shown in the CSR models.

Since our discussion here focuses on the diffusion, adaptation, and integration of ACL practices, we introduce here the key concepts of institutional theory in the context of organizations. Institutional theory is a central growing paradigm in the sociology of organizations. It focuses on several themes of the main concepts and outcomes of research (e.g., institutional logics, institutional work, and isomorphism), but for our purpose, we introduce and incorporate the most relevant themes.

We claim that an institutional perspective to ACL should focus on three main elements. First, it is the process of diffusing key elements from other organizations operating in the business sector into universities. Applying an open system perspective, where changes in organizational environments have an impact on organizational processes and decision-making, it is clear that organizations impact each other and that norms, practices, and logics transcend organizational boundaries (Drori et al., 2006). Such diffusion processes operate also between various organizational forms, allowing the norms and practices in market corporations to move to NGOs and universities. These diffusion processes call for understanding the possible translation of the key elements from markets and business organizations to the operational functioning of universities (Gallardo-Vázquez and Sanchez-Hernandez, 2014).

Second, we need to understand the organizational practices and routines associated with CSR (Matten and Moon, 2008). This means that if there is a diffusion of CSR practices into universities, we need to see how they can be adapted to the mission context and roles of universities. Third, the literature on CSR has argued that a corporation's adoption of social responsibility practices is associated with the aim to enhance organizational legitimacy in society (Matten and Moon, 2008). Thus, organizational legitimacy is an important concept with regards to both CSR and ACL.

The question arising from these claims, in the context of ACL, is about the degree to which universities' adoption of social responsibility practices is associated with the same aim of gaining legitimacy and whether the outcome of legitimacy for universities is similar in meaning to the one gained by market corporations (Garriga and Melé, 2004).

By adopting the lenses of institutional theory, we can sort out various institutional conditions that will act as contextual variables, either enhancing or limiting organizational or individual interest in establishing social responsibility routines. For profit-making market corporations, there are many reasons to act with social responsibility. The past two decades have shown a wide range of publications demonstrating that corporations engage in many social responsibility activities, including giving to charities, supporting community activities, treating employees and customers decently, and maintaining standards of integrity, transparency, and honesty (Campbell, 2007). We now wish to turn to question the comparison between CSR and ACL elements.

In Table 3.1, we compare the basic elements of CSR and ACL. The main components of this comparison include the advancement of public goods and social missions; the direction of organizational processes; the relations of these socially related elements to the other missions of the organization; the institutionalization of practices and the socialization of new organizational entrants with them; and the main stakeholders involved in this mission.

## FROM CSR TO ACL: BETWEEN TRANSLATION AND INNOVATION

We have seen the influence of the CSR framework on any organization's strategy for engaging with and having an impact on its social context. Now, we ask, what may this impact be for universities and institutions of higher education? How is ACL distinct from other forms of social engagement of the university throughout its millennium-long history? In our effort to conceptualize ACL, we discuss herein the differences

Table 3.1    Comparing basic elements of CSR and ACL

|  | CSR | ACL |
|---|---|---|
| Advancing public good and social missions | An additional formal goal of for-profit organizations | An additional informal goal of academic organizations |
| Directions of processes | Top-down – a managerial approach | Mainly bottom-up and some top-down – an entrepreneurial approach |
| Relation to the other missions | Not tightly specified, yet inspired by the phrase "going well by doing good" | In conjuncture with the teaching, research, or technology transfer/ entrepreneurship missions |
| Institutionalizing practices and socializing new entrants | Based on the managerial conception and practices in each firm | Based on a conjuncture between the scholars and scientists in the institution and the management spirit with regards to social involvement |
| Main stakeholders | Other businesses, NGOs, and the general public | Other universities, students, the state, and different groups in need |

between ACL and the university's derivation of the three missions and the basic assertions for the need for ACL.

While the spirit of CSR is unitary – namely, the involvement of corporations and for-profit organizations in, and contribution to, projects that promote social good – the interpretation of CSR is varied: from care for environmental degradation, to labour and employment practices, to neighbourhood watch and educational initiatives. In this regard, the influence of CSR on any initiative to promote social good, especially in universities, is complicated by the miscellany of the CSR model and the ambiguity of CSR's definition.

Consequently, the following are important questions to raise regarding the possibility of having the university's social mission influenced by CSR: what might a new vision for academia's impact on social good be like? What goal or path should the university set for itself to promote social good in the context of the 21st century? This book proposes a process model that can be of value in the context where elements of the fourth mission of ACL are adopted. For this purpose, it is important to account for some basic assumptions regarding the adaptability of this model.

First, since universities are compositions of experts, knowledge, and capabilities that are somewhat idiosyncratic, it is important not to offer a singular model but rather propose an adaptive model. This model can account for differences in interests and goals, both on the individual and the organizational levels, regarding possible leadership and responsibility directions.

Second, following this first assertion, it is important to develop a model that is both bottom-up and top-down, where there is a great deal of alertness to individual academicians and their preferences or conceptions and to directions that are proposed by the university leadership in general. It is important to develop task teams composed of various academic scholars from different fields and of central administrators that will discuss possible directions, their relevance and importance for the university, and their applicability to the public or social world around them.

Third, it is important to take a risky learning approach that allows for failures and hurdles so that various actions and directions can be explored. In this context, more than in any other area, our view is that it is important to assume the nonlinearity of change processes and to allow several parallel processes to emerge and be evaluated after a certain period.

Our suggested change, learning, and adaptation model is based on Crossan et al. (2011). They offered a review and reflection on theories of organizational learning. As they argued, the concept of organizational learning is so complex and varies in context and interpretation, and it is important to offer clear model specifications, with a multi-level approach, various direct and mixed effects, and moderators. They argue for a homologous model that is both parsimonious and powerful.

As we have indicated above, in our view of university-based organizational change (different from individual initiatives that can be taken by individual academicians), the suggested change model should be both bottom-up and top-down. In the bottom-up process, we refer to an interactive process in which various interested university agents come up with suggestions, ideas, and projects. These possible directions must be emergent and interactive with no constraining, higher level forces. The ideas have to follow intuitions that can be based on past experience, cognition, effect, or introspective questioning. Following Crossan et al. (2011), this stage will produce the "raw material of emergence" (p. 457). These loosely connected materials are generated and become the building blocks for the emergence of nonlinear organizational learning negotiations. The model assumes that when the interested academic agents are fully committed to the process, the learning process will start and become an innovative power of emergence.

Mapping the suggested model, based on Crossan et al. (2011), we offer a framework that offers the basis of an innovative organizational change and learning process. The model is based on a processual epistemology, similar to the one offered by Weick (1979) of variation–selection–retention. This process will combine the individual, group, and organizational levels through a process of ideas, possible projects, combinations, resources, and constraints.

## ACL: PROPOSAL FOR AN INNOVATIVE NOVEL MISSION FOR THE UNIVERSITY

In our effort to conceptualize ACL, and to distinguish it from the three canonized missions of universities, we offer here answers to four key questions: Why? What? Who? and How? Table 3.2 summarizes this comparative approach, comparing ACL with other university missions that constitute a logic for university engagement with, and impact on, society and that organize university activities towards such missions.

The first question is "Why?" Why ACL? Why is it needed? Why should universities depart from their traditional roles and incorporate ACL activities into their well-established traditional activities? The university's first mission – teaching – explains that the social role of universities is delivering human knowledge to students and, with that, expanding human capital. Even though teaching at the medieval university was mostly based on religious texts, the overarching logic still remains. This is despite the fact that the language of human capital enhancement comes from the 20th century, when skilling at the tertiary educational level became relevant for production roles. Teaching is a form of diffusion of academic knowledge, and the spread of such knowledge enhances social capacity. The university's second mission – research – explains the social role of universities in the expansion of human knowledge. It is therefore related to the 19th-century humanist secularization, the institutionalization of the scientific method, and, with them, the abandonment of religious or otherwise sacred texts as the sources of knowledge.

The second question is "What?" Assuming there is rationale for developing ACL and that the answer for the first question is a positive one, we can move on to ask, what are the possible forms of academia's social role? Also, what are the relations between ACL and the traditional definitions of academia's social role? Here too, the three primary aca-

Table 3.2 Perspectives on the social impact of universities: positioning academic leadership and responsibility (ACL)

|  | Traditional perspective | | Emerging perspective |
|---|---|---|---|
|  | Teaching | Research | Commercialization | ACL as 4th academic mission |
| Why | To deliver human knowledge; to expand human capital | To expand human knowledge | To satisfy societal needs through cooperation with the industry and government | To engage with society at large; to drive social and human change |
| What | Teaching | Research and teaching for research | Teaching and research in service of needs, with for-profit rationale | Positively impact engagement on voluntary or not-for-profit basis, towards impact on social welfare, social goods, and justice |
| Who | Academicians as teachers | Academicians as researchers | Academicians as entrepreneurs, likely commercial entrepreneurs | Academicians as social leaders |
| How | By applying best practices to deliver knowledge and enhance analytic and critical learning capabilities | By conducting rigorous research aiming to answer challenging research questions while preserving the guidelines of research integrity | By engaging in technology transfer practices that bring knowledge generated in academia to the market for the benefit of society | By volunteering mentorship; public teaching; facilitating social change; establishing university-based NGOs; and conducting public social events |
|  | **Bounded university** | | | **University with porous boundaries** |

demic missions of the university through its history dictate the answers, with teaching, research, and their harnessing towards progress through commercialization governing the social engagement of universities to date. The transition to the ACL model calls for the proactive engagement of universities in a variety of social agendas, with particular attention to social welfare and justice. Here rest two important distinctions between the entrepreneurial university and ACL model. The first and most important distinction is regarding the target of responsibility: moving from expecting that the university's engagement with the government or industry will "trickle down" and thus focusing on bringing social change to all social strata and a variety of spheres, as is the presupposition of the third mission, as well as orienting the university towards explicitly impacting social welfare and justice. The second distinction between the third mission and ACL is in the role taken by academicians: from working from their "lab" outwards, meaning carrying their academic knowledge to impact society, as is assumed by the entrepreneurial university model, to adding a social impact agenda to their professional role alongside their teaching, research, and development-oriented entrepreneurship. On this point, ACL applies to individual academicians and to higher education, science, and academic organizations; it is a call for persons and systems to drive personal action and organizational practices.

The third question – "Who?" – further specifies the defined role of academicians, both individuals and organizations. In addition to focusing on their professional role as teachers, researchers, and/or entrepreneurs – in line with the first, second, and third academic missions, respectively – the ACL model calls for academicians and universities to be defined as social leaders. Moreover, as noted earlier, the conceptual foundation is the definition of academicians as social actors, implying a high level of personal and organizational agency. It does not, however, assume singular action but rather encourages collaboration – that is, inter-organizational partnerships, group support for individuals' projects, and mentorship of young academicians towards this new dimension of their future academic career.

Consequently, the fourth question – "How?" – drives the discussion of strategies for ACL implementation and the process of building the skills and capacity necessary for ACL. How do academic organizations constitute practices that promote ACL's spirit and integrate ACL into new or revised organizational goals, tasks, and procedures? How can academicians be inspired by ACL and then enhance their abilities to integrate it into their professional lives in the university? How can universities legitimize ACL activities, both internally and externally? Also, of course, how are academicians and universities implementing ACL and acting in its spirit? Among these strategies could be the following: volunteering mentorship of social agenda initiatives; public teaching; establishing university-based NGOs; conducting public social events; and more. In the following chapters, we describe several proposals for ACL strategies and illustrate these with examples of academic leadership and commitments by academicians and academic organizations.

By answering these four questions, we define ACL as a novel model for the university's engagement with and impact on society. ACL offers a unique definition for the university's social role, which is appropriate for the current era and the diversity of challenges set before the institution of science and higher education. ACL describes universities based on three main pathways that are described in Chapter 4:

1. Universities as social integrators, namely that universities serve as sites for diverse social groups and minds to come together;
2. Universities as a greenhouse of social leadership by mentoring, expectation-setting, and socialization, namely that universities act as sites for the socialization and empowerment of not only the social elite but the diverse social groups; and,
3. Universities as institutions generating diffusion spillover, namely that universities promote the impactful diffusion of ideas, practices, and tools from their classrooms and labs.

These dimensions of ACL – whether separately or in conjunction – set different directions for the structuration and implementation of ACL. As O'Riordan and Fairbrass (2008) discussed in regard to CSR, it is possible that the multiplicity of ACL pathways creates conflicting expectations and contextual complexities that will challenge ACL. Nevertheless, the overarching theme – that universities are committed to making social impact and to realizing their role as leaders in benefiting public good – maintains the unity of this fourth mission of the university. We devote the following chapters to exploring such paths: in Chapter 4, we provide a broad survey of academic initiatives that exemplify ACL, as well as offer an analytic categorization for ACL approaches and initiatives; in Chapter 5, we describe the Hoffman programme at the Hebrew University of Jerusalem, which was conceived and led by the first author, Amalya Oliver-Lumerman, as a prime example for an ACL initiative; and Chapter 6 outlines examples for ACL-type projects that sprung out of the Hoffman programme at the Hebrew University of Jerusalem. Together, the following three chapters define, describe, and explain what we promote as the model for reorienting the social role of the 21st-century university – namely, academic commitment, and leadership.

> Science, by itself, provides no panacea for individual, social, and economic ills. It can be effective in the national welfare only as a member of a team, whether the conditions be peace or war. But without scientific progress no amount of achievement in other directions can insure our health, prosperity, and security as a nation in the modern world. (Vannevar Bush, *Science – The Endless Frontier*, Report to the US President Roosevelt, July 1945)

## NOTES

1. A simple Google search conducted in January 2020 yielded about 572,000 articles on the topic.
2. http://www.wbcsd.org/work-program/business-role/previous-work/corporate-social-responsibility.aspx.
3. http://ec.europa.eu/enterprise/policies/sustainable-business/corporate-social-responsibility/index_en.htm.
4. http://www.international.gc.ca/trade-agreements-accords-commerciaux/ds/csr.aspx.

# 4. Academic commitment and leaderships: types and examples

With corporate social responsibility (CSR) serving as an embodiment of the new form of social engagement expected of organizations, the 21st-century university is wrestling with the translation of this model to academia. As a result, phrases such as "stakeholder involvement" and "self-regulation" are nowadays added to the vocabulary of university senates, presidents, and programme managers, alongside the traditional concerns of universities with the impact of their teaching, research, and market-related missions, as well as their established initiatives to expand access to higher education (e.g., affirmative action) and to commercialize academic knowledge (aka technology transfer).

As we argued in previous chapters, whereas CSR indeed inspires the recent move in academia to reconsider its social role, universities stand as a unique sector in this regard because universities were constituted out of engagement with society and have, over the millennium-long history of the institution, been redefined through its ever-changing understanding of academia's social role. Therefore, academic commitment and leadership (ACL), the model we propose here as a new direction for social engagement and impact of universities, builds on the longstanding academic tradition of social impact and still reorients it towards the contemporary set of social institutions and the contemporary "grand challenges".

Seeing the commitment to, and leadership of, social causes as distinct from the focus on economic or technological development (which stands firmly as the core of academia's third mission), we define ACL as orienting academic commitment towards the advancement of the public good and fostering leadership of social change as a distinct and yet integral goal of academic education (see also Chapter 2). Moreover, ACL is driven by academicians and scientists; hence, it is a "bottom-up" model for responsibility for the public good: academia's leaders and managers may institutionalize practices that encourage ACL themes and establish ACL programmes. Nevertheless, ACL demands the socialization of academicians to pledge themselves to the advancement and protection of the public good.

## CONTEMPORARY VARIETIES, WITH A LONG HISTORY

Academia's long history revolves around the engagement of the university with society; this is, as we argued previously, at the root of the historiographic ordering of the university's millennium-long transformation around its missions – teaching, research, and commercialization. Along this long route of historical transformation, universities and academicians alike influenced – consciously and unwittingly, directly and implicitly – society and the public good. The variety of historical and locational contexts, coupled with the various degrees of intentionality and multiplicity of social objectives, results in a rich depository of exemplary tales of ACL. Exploring this variety, as we do in the following section, helps clarify ACL's definition.

How are universities strategically contributing to the public good? How are universities benefitting the general public as a form of expressing academic commitment and leadership? In Table 4.1, we list several strategies of ACL, alongside examples of the implementation of such strategies by universities.

The first exemplary strategy is driven by a university's location, where the university engages with the communities that reside in its physical vicinity. Recognized by the phrase "town and gown" (see Miller, 1963), which figuratively describes the relations between the town's residents and the students and faculty members who are recognized by their academic gowns. The strategy acknowledges the social divides between the town's people and academicians: one population is privileged by academic education, whereas the other is not necessarily so; one is transient and arranged by affiliation to its homeland "nations", whereas the other is permanently established in this locale; and one is considered a consumer while the other is regarded as the service provider. These visible social divides were the source of more formal relations, which were frequently adversarial: (1) on more than one occasion, universities leveraged their reputation and impact on the service sector of the town to pressure the town's people for privileges and accommodations, in taxation or land use; and (2) on more than one occasion, town authorities intervened when they judged that university activities were wreaking havoc on residents' orderly life. Interestingly, the strategy that harks back to days when academicians were distinctly attired remains most relevant to the role universities play in urban planning.

The history of the tension between town and gown is long and rich: for example, striving for autonomy from local church authorities and thus manoeuvring between royal patrons, the medieval University of Lisbon, which was founded in Portugal in 1288, migrated several times between the cities of Coimbra and Lisbon before permanently relocating to Coimbra in 1537. Likewise, albeit driven by student protests rather than university leadership, the 1229 conflict between city merchants and later city guardsmen, as well as students of the University of Paris, deteriorated into a student strike and resulted in the scattering of students to other European universities and the closure of this renowned medieval university for two years. Only then, Pope Gregory IX issued the *Parens Scientiarum* bull ("The Mother of Sciences" papal decree; see McKeon, 1964) that guaranteed the University of Paris independence from the local authority and its right to self-governance.

Modern-day universities wrestle with similar issues, and both town and university leaders, hoping to turn the derogatory connotation of the phrase "town and gown" into a mutually agreeable partnership, reconfigure the challenges of authority and domain (den Heijer and Curvelo Magdaniel, 2018). One such domain is that of urban development, with universities involving themselves in urban revitalization schemes: in 2018, Colby College turned the closed industrial mills in downtown Waterville, in the state of Maine in the US, into new student dormitories, thus enlivening a decayed and yet central neighbourhood; likewise, Istanbul's Bilgi University built its largest campus, Silahtarağa campus, into the buildings that were the first power station of the Ottoman Empire, thus taking charge of the early 2000s' redevelopment of this historical site and establishing various scientific and cultural events with the neighbourhood children.

Other city–university partnerships have taken a more formal step, integrating university representatives and student interns into municipal departments and administrative functions. For example, for several years now, the University of Göttingen (Georg-August-Universität Göttingen) in Germany has a university representative in the office of the mayor, facilitating cooperation between "town" and "gown" on issues such as traffic control, housing, skills development, and social justice, which equally burden both city and university leadership. Similarly, Newcastle University was the first to appoint a "dean of place" in 2019 to better engage the university with the specific challenges of England's northeast region. As a final example, the Hebrew University on Mt. Scopus established teaching activities for the youth at the adjacent Palestinian village offering them free of charge as well as preparatory courses that increased their entry scores for admission. In addition, some such initiatives go beyond the city scope to encompass regional and national spaces (see chapters in Hladchenko and Pinheiro, 2019; Pinheiro et al., 2012). For example, Israel's 1994 "college revolution", which challenged the monopoly of research universities and the related social closure of academia, drove colleges into the country's geographical periphery by incentivizing the founding of colleges in rural and geographically remote areas of the country, thus better distributing opportunities outside the core. With these various initiatives, academia is recognizing its place-based responsibilities, alongside the related opportunities.

A second exemplary ACL strategy of universities is to volunteer "academic labour" of both students and faculty members in the service of the general public. In such cases, universities and academicians use their academic skills, resources, and capacities towards social, non-academic goals and, importantly, they do so free of charge. Their volunteer work may take the form of teaching or research, as well as offering their facilities and other resources for public use. However, whereas faculty teach "in exchange" for tuition, students intern in public agencies in exchange for academic credit, and universities rent out their halls for private events for fee. Their ACL strategy is that academic teaching and research skills, as well as facilities and other resources, are endowed on the public without expectations for compensation or reward. In this spirit, academicians volunteer to teach a class in elementary and secondary schools, bringing their science to age groups and communities where attainment of higher education is scant; they volunteer with civic associations and community groups, lending their expertise and stature towards advancing these NGOs' goals, sometimes also voluntarily serving in official capacities for these NGOs.

A related exemplary ACL practice of universities is the "clinics", which are university programmes in which students offer their professional services to the public pro bono. University clinics offer students hands-on experience in their future vocation, while also allowing the public to access professional – un-credentialled but nevertheless supervised by faculty members – guidance that is otherwise out of their reach. Most law schools integrate "public interest centres" (aka clinics) into their legal studies programmes, mostly focusing on those legal matters that would be relevant in low-income communities, such as civil rights and disabilities, family law and domestic violence, housing and social benefits, employment protections, or bankruptcy (see Greenwald, 2007). Such university clinics are also common in other university-based professional schools (i.e., medical, nursing, or dental schools) as well as psychological counselling and social services. The demarking line between the various types of university-based clinics is that clients commonly pay the cost of materials required for treatments or consultations in the health-related fields. Professional academic labour is gratis, yet the university does not charge for the "hard" costs; for example, it covers the costs of labour and expertise but not materials. This demarcation defines the scope of the practice of this ACL strategy: not only what areas and issues are worthy of a university programme for pro bono professional services, but also what components of the "service" are sponsored by the university and what are the responsibilities of the "client".

Going a step further in expressing academic commitment and leadership – from advocacy for social change to action towards such social change – the legitimacy of academicians is translated into a call for social change. Social change sets yet another exemplary practice of ACL. Lending not only their credentials and expertise but rather mostly exploiting their prestige, both universities and individual academicians validate and promote social causes. Moreover, their endorsement is what transforms the social cause into a newsworthy item, widely spreading the call to protect or promote the public good.

There are plenty of examples for this manner of university and academic influence on the social agenda. Famous among them is the impact that the Russell–Einstein Manifesto, which was issued in 1955 by the two renowned Nobel Prize laureates and nine other world-famous scientists, had on the consolidation of the anti-nuclear movement during the years of the Cold War.

However, it is surely true that not all social causes that are advocated by renowned scientists, even those that meet the Nobel Prize criterion of benefitting all of mankind, are deemed by all as significant, beneficial, or just. For example, William Shockley, who shared in the 1956 Nobel Prize in physics for his joint research "on semiconductors and their discovery of the transistor effect" and whose Stanford University professorship sprung the semiconductor industry of Silicon Valley, used his reputation to advocate for the racist ideas known as eugenics, calling for sterilization of the "genetically disadvantaged" and warning against "retrogressive evolution" of having the intellectually superior whites reproduce slower than other "races" (see Shurkin, 2006). With that, and other examples, it is clear that academic reputation does not validate the merit of the social cause that is being advocated for; nevertheless, the social cause benefits from the renown of individual academics and universities.

Still, the ACL practice of academia advocating for social causes remains valuable, even if the public recognition of leading scientists is overshadowed by celebrities. Today, the common venues for expressing such an academic voice on public affairs are op-ed articles written by renowned academics, petitions, and demonstrations by student and faculty groups, as well as court appeals launched by university experts, commonly on behalf of an otherwise silenced social group or neglected cause.

With universities amassing resources, their influence over the public good as economy players grows, and this offers universities another opportunity to act on their academic commitment and leadership. The related ACL strategy requires that universities reorient their profit-making activities towards the protection and expansion of the public good.

Consequently, when negotiating arrangements with industry for joint R&D, accepting donations from generous benefactors, or making investment decisions for their endowments, universities are in a position to steer their market relations according to contemporary social sensibilities or publicly acceptable criteria of ethics and morality. Here, private or otherwise well-endowed universities find themselves in a bind: on the one hand, they need to grow their assets so as to fund their expanding academic ambitions, and on the other hand, they are compelled by the normative frameworks of public science. Such universities carefully walk a "tightrope" between the dependence on yields from their net worth and the promise of academic freedom of study, debate, research, expression, and publication. Therefore, universities structurally separate between these two often-conflicting demands: Harvard Management Company (founded in 1974), Princeton University Investment Company (PRINCO; founded in 1987), and Stanford Management Company (founded 1991) were founded as university subsidiaries. These subsidiaries are charged with managing these universities' assets and endowments in order to financially support each university's educational and research missions and operate in light of formal university proclamations of adherence to investment ethics.

While such proclamations remain somewhat vague on the specific issues that are recognized as abhorrent, they do much to recognize the need for a balance between financial vitality and academic norms. For example, the 2018 version of Stanford University's Statement on

Investment Responsibility, which was initially drafted in 1971 and amended several times since, does more to separate the financial fiduciary responsibilities from the university missions than to define clear ethical criteria. While clearly describing the mechanics of decision-making on ethical investment, it also lists the responsibilities of the university's board of trustees, its advising committees, related offices, guideline documents, and procedures of consultation and appeal. In terms of naming actual social agenda items, the Stanford University statement goes on to specify only the most egregious issues. Among the issues "so abhorrent and ethically unjustifiable as to warrant the University's dissociation from those investments", it includes "apartheid, genocide, human trafficking, slavery, and violations of child labor laws".

In all such steps taken by universities to become "ethical investors", the imprint of CSR is most evident: while public universities, dependent on funding decisions made by elected representatives, find themselves sensitive to the public's priorities, private universities that are thought to be financially autonomous are at least as open to public scrutiny of the ethical and moral standards of their fiscal management. Either way, the few reviews of university investment standards show no inclination towards impact-directed investment: to date, universities have adopted a "do no harm" investment strategy rather than institutionalize a proactive agenda-setting policy. Steering universities in such a direction would require the will of both university leaders and managers – that is, to scrutinize the sources of donations, to consult with a variety of university stakeholders on ethical and moral standards for investments of their endowments, to seek investment venues that aim to increase social impact, and the like. It would require a change to the balance between their position as players in the economy and their public role as academic institutions.

In numerous cases, the commitment and leadership of universities on matters of current social concern, if not of social urgency, are far less contested. For one, the transition of universities to sustainable practices in their own administration affords them much credibility to speak on behalf of society's grand challenges. Ramakrishna et al. (2020) described the role of universities in the transition from the produce–use–throw (linear) economy to a circular economy, which is organized around sustainable systems of operations, production, management, and business, as well as drawing on renewable or recycled resources. Examples from Singapore and South Africa show that universities are well positioned to differentiate themselves as forward thinking and as exemplars in relation to the coming circular economy, namely that universities serve as "living laboratories" for experimentation with those "industry 4.0" technologies, nowadays the cutting-edge technologies of the Internet of Things (IoT), artificial intelligence (AI), and nanotechnology. Through the many channels by which a university impacts and engages with the society in which it is embedded, local and global alike, its commitment and leadership to a sustainable present for the sake of a prosperous and just future make, and could further establish, the role of universities in driving the shift towards CE futures even more central.

Also, if universities themselves hesitate to commit to a positive social impact, "third party" organizations can drive them in such a direction. Therefore, the last exemplary ACL strategy we describe here – valorizing social impact action of universities – is exclusively directed by social actors from outside universities. Currently, we observe two ACL practices that valorize the positive social impact of universities: university ranking and funding schemes. Starting in 2019, the European Commission launched its Horizon Impact Award: research projects that received FP-7 or Horizon 2020 funding are eligible for additional recognition for the "use of their results to provide value for society". This award is supposed to encourage scientists to consider the uptake that the results of their study may have for the general public; it is also supposed to encourage the public to seek social yield from academic research.

Also starting in 2019, the *Times Higher Education* (THE) journal, which produces one of the few reputed global university rankings for academic excellence, issued a new ranking of universities by their performance towards the social goals encoded as the United Nations' Sustainable Development Goals (SDGs). THE's University Impact Ranking scores and then ranks hundreds of universities from tens of countries on, for example, their work towards promoting peace, justice, and strong institutions (SDG 16), gender equality and women's empowerment (SDG 5), good health and well-being (SDG 3), decent work and employment growth (SDG 8), reduced inequalities (SDG 10), and climate action (SDG 13).[1] These valorization practices do not prioritize social impact over scientific excellence; they also do not demand that every university, research project, and academician deliver social impact. They do, however, solidly position social impact among the criteria for academic worth and thus appreciation. This is done by noting social benefits to the general public among the praiseworthy deliverables of academic research and teaching. In this way, they harness "soft law" to drive compliance of universities to the newly recognized performance standards of ACL. In other words, while these governance instruments do not have any legally binding force, they clearly set a new regime of conduct for academia and act to drive changes in academic governance and culture in accordance with this new regime.

Both examples of ACL valorization strategies have only broad definitions of social impact; they are also ambiguous about the uptake of research into social impact or the link between academic performance and its social deliveries; and both example strategies also reveal that this is a recent trend that is still too young to be assessed for its own impact on changing academic priorities. However, following the apparent impact that other funding criteria and rankings had on the practice of science, the governance of the university, and the choices of individual academics, it is clear that these soft law strategies are sure to further drive universities into modes of ACL.

Our list of ACL strategies, described in this chapter and summarized in Table 4.1, is surely not exhaustive; our list is suggestive of pathways taken to date or worthy of further attention, both analytically and in practice. In addition, the categorization, as well as the exemplar strategies and specific tales, somewhat "flatten" the historical development of university–society relations; we select from a variety of eras and locales and thus assemble exemplars across time-space divides. This variety is meant to inspire, as much as it is to analytically describe, ACL.

Taking the analytic-cum-illustrative view to define ACL offered here (Table 4.1) affords a novel way to also rethink the university's other missions, although these were described as attached to the political, economic, and cultural contexts of specific historic eras. In other words, we propose the importance of applying the perspective of ACL – of building academic commitment to the advancement of the public good and fostering leadership of social change – to the academic missions of teaching, research, and commercialization. In Table 4.2, we list several academic practices that orient teaching, research, and commercialization towards the social good and public impact. The point here is not merely to continue viewing teaching, research, and commercialization as "business as usual" but rather to rethink these "traditional" academic missions of the university in the spirit of ACL. Included here are expressions of academic commitment to the public good combined with strategies for academic leadership towards social change, as well as bottom-up initiatives alongside organizational programmes. Also, rather than treating these academic practices as acts of charity, they are seen as acts inherent to

Table 4.1  Varieties of ACL as the fourth academic mission of the university

| Mission of the university | Strategy | Principles |
|---|---|---|
| 4. Academic Commitment and Leadership | Place-based responsibilities | • Change the derogatory meaning of "town and gown" to collaborative urban planning<br>• Offer city–university partnership in urban development projects, thus ensuring university involvement in municipal affairs<br>• Expand the university's spatial commitment: from campus to city to region<br>• Provide initiatives that target neighbouring communities |
| | Volunteering academic skills and resources | • Use academic – teaching and research, teaching – as well as university resources, skills towards social, non-academic goals<br>• Offer pro bono services, free of charge!<br>• Involve both students and faculty, as well as the university as an organization |
| | Civic and political activism | • Advocacy and action towards social change<br>• Involve the university as an organization (programmes such as "clinics" or public interest centres), as well as students and faculty (op-ed articles, demonstrations, petitions, court appeals, and so on) |
| | Market relations with new sensibilities | • Reorient profit-making activities according to publicly discussed criteria<br>• Ensure relevance for both university–industry arrangements and investments of university endowments |
| | Valorizing "social impact" | • Rank universities by their "social impact" (alongside the now common university ranking by academic excellence)<br>• Provide "soft law" mechanisms (standards, rankings, awards) that celebrate (and in doing so also codify) the impact of basic research<br>• Involve "third-party" actors, such as associations or higher education journals |

Table 4.2  ACL themes in the university's first, second, and third academic missions

| Mission of the university | Strategy | Principles |
|---|---|---|
| 1. Teaching | Expanding the reach | Bring advanced education to social groups |
| | Expanding the scope | Academize issues that are subject to public debate |
| | Adding ethics to curricula | Affect students' values and behaviour and change their impression of their role in society for life |
| 2. Research | Social impact and deliveries | Assess research in regard to its social impact and deliveries, in policy, while also maintaining scientific excellence |
| | Addressing the neglected | Direct research towards social issues that are unprofitable for private research or overlooked by public policy |
| 3. Commercialization | Tech creation, for social aims | Provide non-proprietary creation of research-driven technology, made for public use |
| | Market relations | Allow for investments and yields (through, for example, sales and leasing of properties), with profit motives justified as reinvestments |
| | Curricula and teaching | Provide uniquely academic products (such as courses, textbooks and lectures) for public use, also without charge |

academia of the 21st century. These ACL principles require that teaching, research, and commercialization be revised at least on some dimensions.

Orienting the academic mission of teaching towards the delivery of benefits to the general public means expanding the reach of teaching or expanding its scope. The expansion of academic teaching pertains to bringing advanced or higher education to social groups that are otherwise excluded from access to such education. This aim is at the root of such initiatives that are committed to reaching out to wider social groups; it is also the underlying rationale for the founding of the Open University model, which was first established in the UK in 1969 and subsequently diffused worldwide. This model institutionalized a new format for research universities that offered lower entry thresholds and distance learning.

Expanding the scope of the academic mission of teaching means educating students about issues that are marginalized in public discussions: today, we are no longer astonished by the academic study of global warming or social inequality; likewise, academic teaching does and should continue to highlight society's grand challenges, local, and global.

Teaching also has the power to affect students' values and behaviour and, with that, redraw their future relation to society's grand challenges. Through curricular and pedagogical tools, academic teaching not only provides knowledge about societal conditions and challenges but also sets these as priorities and building commitment to solving societal problems. Such teaching-driven and student-focused initiatives for changing hearts are already in practice in professional university schools. In business education, for example, business ethics courses were introduced as an integral part of the business curriculum in the hope of swaying future managers to be attuned to social needs and goals, to commit to social action and impact, and to lead the organizations that they must manage in a manner that is respectful of societal conditions and the public good. Murcia et al. (2018), in debating the purpose, content, and outcomes of university-level management education, advocated for the "Athenian paradigm" over the "Spartan paradigm": they argued for the "dominance of an instrumental, Spartan paradigm in management education, which has a number of short-term benefits but over the longer term leads to a gradual erosion of common good" (Murcia et al., 2018, p. 589). In its place, they advocated for the Athenian model, which replaces the mission of maximizing short-term agent gains with the mission of harmonizing among multiple societal stakeholders, replaces the methods of abstract modelling with the pedagogy of engagement and experiential learning, and replaces specialist faculty with socially-minded leaders.

Similarly, research can further be aimed at society's grand challenges, not only as the object of study but also by adding social deliverables to research. In other words, academic research – even beyond "applied" research or "basic" research – is and could be assessed on its engagement with the general public or its direct social impact. This can be done by drafting policy papers, creating social programmes that build on insights from research, or communicating research findings to the general public. Also, in regard to neglected spheres of research, academic research could investigate and innovate wherever the motives of the private or governmental sectors are absent.

In such cases, the academic mission of knowledge production and commercialization could also be steered by ACL strategies to create research outputs, even technology and devices, to address social challenges and meet social goals with non-proprietary strings attached. In such cases, the creation of research-driven technology is designed for public needs. Since even public universities increasingly require registration and admission fees for accessing their resources, including courses and libraries, teaching too is becoming a profit-generating mechanism for universities, and the ACL-themed commercialization mission could also drive universities further into granting public use of its curricula.

Overall, it is clear that universities already wrestle with their public role and thus have been and still are fulfilling their academic missions with public needs and challenges in mind. Still, as we argue throughout this book, ACL regards these academic norms and related practices as inherent features of contemporary science and academia. It is also made clear that extending these first, second, and third academic missions of universities (namely teaching, research, and commercialization) demands academic freedoms – that is, of thought, debate, and expression. To be able to identify neglected social concerns and make them the focus of study, academicians must be liberated from political or economic pressures.

## THE ROLE OF ACL MODELS: EINSTEIN AS THE ICONIC SCIENTIST–ACTIVIST

One of the principal features of ACL is that it is a bottom-up form of commitment and leadership; of those socially privileged by academia and from academia, it is a type of social activism. In other words, the point is not leading others in the act itself but setting expectations, making an impact, and, with that, leading towards protection of the public good. In themselves, they create a legacy, and such a legacy promotes the act of leadership.

Can we consider those practicing ACL academicians as innovators or institutional entrepreneurs? The answer is, no – or, rather, not necessarily. Institutional entrepreneurs are defined in the organizational literature as organized actors who envision new institutional arrangements and advance the interests, and the values that are suppressed by the existing logics of the institution (DiMaggio, 1988; Greenwood and Suddaby, 2006). Much like entrepreneurs and innovators, they can envision a project and start it by leading an initiative in the hope that something grander will evolve out of it and thus deliver social impact. Like institutional entrepreneurs, ACL academicians can change an institution – either the institution that their initiative targets or academia itself. Still, they do not necessarily have to manage the operation of an ongoing entrepreneurial initiative since their actions are signals of commitment and leadership. In the next illustrative case, we describe the example of Einstein as an institutional entrepreneur of ACL.

Albert Einstein did not perceive himself as a social leader or activist, yet he did take a serious and important public stand on several social issues. With that, his dual role stands as a renowned scientist and as a principled citizen who worked to expand the public good. Thus, Einstein is a prime example of ACL. Moreover, his reputation as scientist-cum-activist marks him as an iconic role model for ACL-ers. In this section, we describe three tales from Einstein's life, including instances and issues where he expressed opinions on public issues and acted publicly with the aim of bringing change to social matters that he deemed important for the general public: Einstein's stand on promoting the rights of African Americans, his action towards pacifism and against the use of nuclear might, and his iconic statement of "The Mission of Our University", which, while written in honour of the founding of the Hebrew University of Jerusalem, speaks to the social role of academia in general. In these three tales of Einstein, we see various ways in which Einstein relied on his fame to advocate for and act on behalf of social causes that benefit the general public.

### Tale 1: Einstein Advocating for the Rights of African Americans in the US

This tale shows Einstein's commitment to alleviating social ills, using his renown to persuade policymakers, community leaders, and the public about social injustice and to encourage them to act on such convictions to remedy social ills. Soon after his arrival to reside in the US, Einstein was driven to act on behalf of the advancement of rights for African Americans, then referred to as American Negros. In a letter dated October 29, 1931, and addressed to the editor of *The Crises* in response to his plea to Einstein to write about the "... evil of race prejudice in the world" (Jerome and Taylor, 2005, p. 135), Einstein replied with the following words:

> It seems to be a universal fact that the minorities, especially when their individuals are recognizable because of physical differences, are treated by majorities among whom they live as an inferior class. The tragic part of such

a faith, however, lies not only on the automatically realized disadvantages suffered by these minorities in economic and social relations, but also the fact that those who meet such treatment themselves for the most part acquiesce in the prejudiced estimate because of the suggestive influence of the majority, and come to regard people like themselves as inferior. This second and more important aspect of the evil can be met through closer union and conscious educational enlightenment among the minority, and so emancipation of the soul of the minority can be attained. The determined effort of the American Negroes in this direction deserves every recognition and assistance. (Jerome and Taylor, 2005, pp. 136–137)

Expressing such social support in the rights of African Americans by acting against prejudice and offering recognition and support is a meaningful ACL act, and when expressed in 1931 by a well-known scientist, it constitutes as important social advocacy and activism. As expressed by the sociologist and civil rights activist, Dr. Du Bois, when he wrote about this letter from Einstein,

A genius in higher physics and ranks with Copernicus, Newton and Kepler. His famous theory of Relativity, advanced first in 1905, is revolutionizing our explanation of physical phenomenon and our conception of Motion, Time and Space. … But Professor Einstein is not a mere mathematical mind. He is a living being sympathetic with all human advance. He is a brilliant advocate of disarmament and world Peace and he hates race prejudice because as a Jew he knows what it is. … (Jerome and Taylor, 2005, p. 136)

In addition to writing advocacy letters on behalf of African Americans, Einstein also expressed his support of African Americans' rights in public. In an address at the Inauguration of the "Wall of Fame" at the World's Fair in New York, 1940, Einstein referred to immigrants and African Americans and called for social integration. In his speech, Einstein proclaimed,[2]

It is a fine and high-minded idea, also in the best sense a proud one, to erect at the World's Fair a wall of fame to immigrants and Negroes of distinction.

The significance of the gesture is this: it says: These too belong to us and we are glad and grateful to acknowledge the debt that the community owes them. And [focusing on] these particular contributors, Negroes and immigrants, shows that the community feels a special need to show regards and affection to those who are often regarded as stepchildren of the nation – for why else this combination?

If, then, I am to speak on the occasion, it can only be to say something in behalf of these stepchildren. As for the immigrants, they are the only ones to whom it can be accounted a merit to be Americans. For they had to take trouble for their citizenship, whereas it has cost the majority nothing at all to be born in the land of civic freedom.

As for the Negroes, the country has still a heavy debt to discharge for all the troubles and disabilities it has laid on the Negro's shoulders, for all this his fellow-citizens have done and to some extent still are doing to him. To the Negro and his wonderful songs and choirs, we are indebted for the finest contribution in the realm of art which America has so far given to the world. And this great gift we owe, not to those whose names are engraved on this "Wall of Fame", but to the children of the people, blossoming namelessly as the lilies in the field. (Jerome and Taylor, 2005, pp. 138–139)

The call for a fight against prejudice and the advancement of minorities' social integration is expressed again in a letter sent on September 16, 1946 to Dr. Lester B. Granger, who is the executive director of the National Urban League, where Einstein wrote the following:

I greet your assembly in the conviction that it deals with one of the most important problems in this country. The contrast among groups is constant threat which imperils minorities. This threat becomes more acute in times of economic stress and insecurity. ... The worst disease under which the society of our nation suffers, is, in my opinion, the treatment of the Negro. Everyone who is not used from childhood to this injustice suffers from the mere observation. Everyone who freshly learns of this state of affairs at a maturer age, feels not only the injustice, but the scorn of the principle of the Fathers who founded the United States that "all men are created equal". ... Today, however, this prejudice is still alive and powerful. The fight against it is difficult as is the fight over every issue in which the enemy has thoughtlessness and a fatal tradition on its side. What is to be done? (Jerome and Taylor, 2005, p. 145)[3]

Further, Einstein suggested a few steps that should be taken:

First, we must make every effort [to ensure] that the past injustice, violence and economic discrimination will be made known to the people; the taboo, the "let's-not-talk-about-it" must be broken. It must be pointed out time and again that the exclusion of a large part of the colored population from active civil rights by common practices is a slap in the face of the Constitution of the nation. We must strive [to ensure] that minorities be protected against economic and political discrimination as well as against attack by libellous writings and against the position of youth in the schools. ... (Jerome and Taylor, 2005, p. 146)

Einstein ended his letter by comparing two possible societies – one characterized by the egotistic enjoyment of beauty and the blooming life, as well as compassion for the suffering, and the other by a moral climate where the value of life has a decisive influence. The final sentence is a strong statement: "One thing is certain: No mechanisms can give us a good moral climate as long as we have not freed ourselves from the prejudices to whose defeat you are devoting yourselves" (Jerome and Taylor, 2005, p. 147).

## Tale 2: The Russell–Einstein Manifesto

This initiative is a collaborative effort of renowned scientists to oppose the use of nuclear weapons and to call for a peaceful use of scientific discoveries, with Einstein placing the weight of his prominence and popularity in support of this initiative. The Manifesto, drafted by Literature Noble Laureate Bertrand Russell and signed by ten additional illustrious scientists, was issued in London in July 1955, in the midst of the Cold War. It posits a moral and ethical alert about the dangers posed to humanity as a whole by nuclear weapons and calls governments to commit to both nuclear freeze and peaceful resolution of interstate conflicts. Declaring the threat and calling for action, the Manifesto concludes with the following resolution:

> In view of the fact that in any future world war nuclear weapons will certainly be employed, and that such weapons threaten the continued existence of mankind, we urge the governments of the world to realise, and to acknowledge publicly, that their purpose cannot be furthered by a world war, and we urge them, consequently, to find peaceful means for the settlement of all matters of dispute between them.[4]

This call for action rests on ethical and moral grounds. The Manifesto speaks in terms of people's concern for their children and grandchildren, humanity's prosperous future rather than the "imminent danger of perishing agonizingly", and peaceful resolution to conflict and aggression – all of which, it is claimed, are made dim by the political and "vague and abstract" use of the term "mankind" and by the rallying call of nationalism. With articulation of these sentiments, the Manifesto became the foundation for the Pugwash movement, starting with its 1957 Conference on Science and World Affairs, and energized many of the signatories to further advocate for scientists' responsibility to serve as a social conscience and to thus guide solutions to social problems (see Rotblat, 1997/2016).

The Manifesto's importance, in addition to advocating for world peace and setting the foundation for the Pugwash movement, is also specific to the social role of scientists in speaking out on behalf of humanity on urgent societal matters. The words of the Manifesto speak loudly on this point. First, the Manifesto sets scientists as the avant-garde, or bold and valiant leadership, of humanity. Second, the Manifesto also assigns scientists a moral and ethical role. Third, it assigns science a universalistic agenda that is free of political or other biases on this urgent and dangerous matter, even if every scientist holds this or that political view.

> We are speaking on this occasion, not as members of this or that nation, continent, or creed, but as human beings, members of the species Man, whose continued existence is in doubt.
>
> We shall try to say no single word which should appeal to one group rather than to another. All, equally, are in peril, and, if the peril is understood, there is hope that they may collectively avert it.

In these ways, the Manifesto speaks to the role of scientists and science in recognizing and alerting against dangers to humanity – more than ever when such dangers are outcomes of scientific discoveries. Therefore, importantly, the Manifesto sets an inextricable link between science, ethics, and morality, and it places scientists as responsible for safeguarding this trust. Therefore, whereas "people will not face this alternative because it is so difficult to abolish war", the Manifesto posits that scientists are custodians and alerts prophets to imminent dangers to the future of humanity, defined here as devastation brought by nuclear war.

---

**BOX 4.1 THE RUSSELL–EINSTEIN MANIFESTO: 9 JULY 1955**

In the tragic situation which confronts humanity, we feel that scientists should assemble in conference to appraise the perils that have arisen as a result of the development of weapons of mass destruction, and to discuss a resolution in the spirit of the appended draft.

We are speaking on this occasion, not as members of this or that nation, continent, or creed, but as human beings, members of the species Man, whose continued existence is in doubt. The world is full of conflicts; and, overshadowing all minor conflicts, the titanic struggle between Communism and anti-Communism.

Almost everybody who is politically conscious has strong feelings about one or more of these issues; but we want you, if you can, to set aside such feelings and consider yourselves only as members of a biological species which has had a remarkable history, and whose disappearance none of us can desire.

We shall try to say no single word which should appeal to one group rather than to another. All, equally, are in peril, and, if the peril is understood, there is hope that they may collectively avert it.

We have to learn to think in a new way. We have to learn to ask ourselves, not what steps can be taken to give military victory to whatever group we prefer, for there no longer are such steps; the question we have to ask ourselves is: what steps can be taken to prevent a military contest of which the issue must be disastrous to all parties?

The general public, and even many men in positions of authority, have not realized what would be involved in a war with nuclear bombs. The general public still thinks in terms of the obliteration of cities. It is understood that the new bombs are more powerful than the old, and that, while one A-bomb could obliterate Hiroshima, one H-bomb could obliterate the largest cities, such as London, New York, and Moscow.

No doubt in an H-bomb war great cities would be obliterated. But this is one of the minor disasters that would have to be faced. If everybody in London, New York, and Moscow were exterminated, the world might, in the course of a few centuries, recover from the blow. But we now know, especially since the Bikini test, that nuclear bombs can gradually spread destruction over a very much wider area than had been supposed.

It is stated on very good authority that a bomb can now be manufactured which will be 2,500 times as powerful as that which destroyed Hiroshima.

Such a bomb, if exploded near the ground or under water, sends radio-active particles into the upper air. They sink gradually and reach the surface of the earth in the form of a deadly dust or rain. It was this dust which infected the Japanese fishermen and their catch of fish.

No one knows how widely such lethal radio-active particles might be diffused, but the best authorities are unanimous in saying that a war with H-bombs might possibly put an end to the human race. It is feared that if many H-bombs are used there will be universal death, sudden only for a minority, but for the majority a slow torture of disease and disintegration.

Many warnings have been uttered by eminent men of science and by authorities in military strategy. None of them will say that the worst results are certain. What they do say is that these results are possible, and no one can be sure that they will not be realized. We have not yet found that the views of experts on this question depend in any degree upon their politics or prejudices. They depend only, so far as our researches have revealed, upon the extent of the particular expert's knowledge. We have found that the men who know most are the most gloomy.

Here, then, is the problem which we present to you, stark and dreadful and inescapable: Shall we put an end to the human race; or shall mankind renounce war?[1] People will not face this alternative because it is so difficult to abolish war.

The abolition of war will demand distasteful limitations of national sovereignty.[2] But what perhaps impedes understanding of the situation more than anything else is that the term "mankind" feels vague and abstract. People scarcely realize in imagination that the danger is to themselves and their children and their grandchildren, and not only to a dimly apprehended humanity. They can scarcely bring themselves to grasp that they, individually, and those whom they love are in imminent danger of perishing agonizingly. And so they hope that perhaps war may be allowed to continue provided modern weapons are prohibited.

This hope is illusory. Whatever agreements not to use H-bombs had been reached in time of peace, they would no longer be considered binding in time of war, and both sides would set to work to manufacture H-bombs as soon as war broke out, for, if one side manufactured the bombs and the other did not, the side that manufactured them would inevitably be victorious.

Although an agreement to renounce nuclear weapons as part of a general reduction of armaments[3] would not afford an ultimate solution, it would serve certain important purposes.

First, any agreement between East and West is to the good in so far as it tends to diminish tension. Second, the abolition of thermo-nuclear weapons, if each side believed that the other had carried it out sincerely, would lessen the fear of a sudden attack in the style of Pearl Harbour, which at present keeps both sides in a state of nervous apprehension. We should, therefore, welcome such an agreement though only as a first step.

Most of us are not neutral in feeling, but, as human beings, we have to remember that, if the issues between East and West are to be decided in any manner that can give any possible satisfaction to anybody, whether Communist or anti-Communist, whether Asian or European or American, whether White or Black, then these issues must not be decided by war. We should wish this to be understood, both in the East and in the West.

There lies before us, if we choose, continual progress in happiness, knowledge, and wisdom. Shall we, instead, choose death, because we cannot forget our quarrels? We appeal as human beings to human beings: Remember your humanity, and forget the rest. If you can do so, the way lies open to a new Paradise; if you cannot, there lies before you the risk of universal death.

**Resolution:**

We invite this Congress, and through it the scientists of the world and the general public, to subscribe to the following resolution:

> In view of the fact that in any future world war nuclear weapons will certainly be employed, and that such weapons threaten the continued existence of mankind, we urge the governments of the world to realize, and to acknowledge publicly, that their purpose cannot be furthered by a world war, and we urge them, consequently, to find peaceful means for the settlement of all matters of dispute between them.

**Signatories:**

Max Born
Percy W. Bridgman
Albert Einstein
Leopold Infeld
Frederic Joliot-Curie
Herman J. Muller
Linus Pauling
Cecil F. Powell
Joseph Rotblat
Bertrand Russell
Hideki Yukawa

**Notes:**

1. Professor Joliot-Curie wishes to add the words: "as a means of settling differences between States".
2. Professor Joliot-Curie wishes to add that these limitations are to be agreed by all and in the interests of all.
3. Professor Muller makes the reservation that this be taken to mean "a concomitant balanced reduction of all armaments".

Author's Note: Footnotes added from Rotblat, J. (Ed.) (1982). *Proceedings of the First Pugwash Conference on Science and World Affairs, Pugwash Council, 1982,* 167–170.

Einstein, who signed the Manifesto days before his death, voiced his concern about nuclear threats to humanity, specifically about the nuclear arms race spurred by the Cold War, on numerous occasions before Russell's initiative to draft the Manifesto. In August 1939, just prior to the outbreak of war in Europe, Einstein and fellow exiled physicist Leó Szilárd sent a letter to US President Roosevelt in which they expressed their alarm about Nazi advances in nuclear research and nuclear armament: the Einstein-Szilárd letter asserts that uranium could be fashioned into "extremely powerful bombs of a new type". Moreover, based on his premonitions regarding Nazi ambitions, Einstein urged President Roosevelt to speed up American efforts in experimental work on nuclear fission; indeed, soon after the war's outbreak and before the US was formally involved, also partly due to Einstein's prompting, the president's Advisory Committee on Uranium was formed in October 1939. Yet, when the US gained nuclear capabilities and the community of physicists started openly wrestling with the overwhelming devastation that such weaponry was tested to inflict – to the point that Joseph Rotblat loudly abandoned the Manhattan Project – Einstein disassociated himself from the Manhattan Project and his pacificist convictions drove him into action again, to protest the military and destructive uses of nuclear might. Later, Einstein is quoted as claiming the following:

> I do not consider myself the father of the release of atomic energy. My part in it was quite indirect. I did not, in fact, foresee that it would be released in my time. I believed only that it was theoretically possible. It became practical through the accidental discovery of chain reaction, and this was not something I could have predicted.[5]

Still, in spite of the complicated connection between discovery and the use of scientific findings, as well as between the basic or theoretical research and applied research, Einstein took responsibility for the role of theoretical physics in the devastation and horror of using nuclear weapons on civilian populations in Japan through action. In May 1946, he became chair of the newly formed Emergency Committee of Atomic Scientists, which propagated a message of peaceful, rather than military and destructive, uses of nuclear energy and subsequently stood firmly alongside Russell with the Manifesto initiative.

**Tale 3: Einstein and "The Mission of Our University"**

Tale 3 most explicitly links Einstein with the social role and impact of the university as the prime organizational form of science and academia. In a public letter published on 27 March 1925 in the *New Palestine* newspaper (vol. 8, no. 13, p. 294; see Box 4.2), Einstein articulated an agenda for the relations between academia and society. The letter, carrying the illustrious title "The Mission of Our University", was published just days before the start of studies at the newly established Hebrew University of Jerusalem. Importantly, the letter set a series of "missions" that, while written for this first Jewish university and first university in the British mandate of Palestine, still resonate with current-day academia. In this sense, the scientist who changed the course of science and was declared "man of the century" has here established the blueprint for academia's social impact also in the 21st century. Indeed, as explained in greater detail in the forthcoming text, the *Magna Charta Universitatum*, which is better known as the Bologna Declaration of 1988 and that launched the Bologna Process of European academic harmonization, affirms the principles articulated in Einstein's open letter over six decades earlier.

> **BOX 4.2 "THE MISSION OF OUR UNIVERSITY": ALBERT EINSTEIN**
>
> The opening of the Hebrew University on Mount Scopus, at Jerusalem, is an event which should not only fill us with just pride, but should also inspire us to serious reflection.
>
> A University is a place where the universality of the human spirit manifests itself. Science and investigation recognize as their aim the truth only. It is natural, therefore, that institutions which serve the in-

terests of science should be a factor making for the union of nations and men. Unfortunately, the universities of Europe to-day are for the most part the nurseries of chauvinism and of a blind intolerance of all things foreign to the particular nation or race, of all things bearing the stamp of a different individuality. Under this regime the Jews are the principal sufferers, not only because they are thwarted in their desire for free participation and in their striving for education, but also because most Jews find themselves particularly cramped in this spirit of narrow nationalism. On this occasion of the birth of our University, I should like to express the hope that our University will always be free from this evil, that teachers and students will always preserve the consciousness that they serve their people best when they maintain its union with humanity and with the highest human values.

Jewish nationalism is today a necessity because only through a consolidation of our national life can we eliminate those conflicts from which the Jews suffer today. May the time soon come when this nationalism will have become so thoroughly a matter of course that it will no longer be necessary for us to give it special emphasis. Our affiliation with our past and with the present-day achievements of our people inspires us with assurance and pride vis-à-vis the entire world. But our educational institutions in particular must regard it as one of their noblest tasks to keep our people free from nationalistic obscurantism and aggressive intolerance.

Our University is still a modest undertaking. It is quite the correct policy to begin with a number of research institutes, and the University will develop naturally and organically. I am convinced that this development will make rapid progress and that in the course of time this institution will demonstrate with the greatest clearness the achievements of which the Jewish spirit is capable. A special task devolves upon the University in the spiritual direction and education of the laboring sections of our people in the land. In Palestine it is not our aim to create another people of city dwellers leading the same life as in the European cities and possessing the European bourgeois standards and conceptions. We aim at creating a people of workers, at creating the Jewish village in the first place, and we desire that the treasures of culture should be accessible to our laboring class, especially since, as we know, Jews, in all circumstances, place education above all things. In this connection it devolves upon the University to create something unique in order to serve the specific needs of the forms of life developed by our people in Palestine.

> All of us desire to cooperate in order that the University may accomplish its mission. May the realization of the significance of this cause penetrate among the large masses of Jewry. Then our University will develop speedily into a great spiritual center which will evoke the respect of cultured mankind the world over.
>
> Albert Einstein, "The Mission of our University", *New Palestine*, 27 March 1925, 13: 294.

Einstein wrote this open letter in his role as member of the board of governors of the Hebrew University, thus honouring the university's opening celebrations in absentia. His statement therefore balanced universalist values with a particularistic agenda set for the Zionist national project. On the one hand, he defined a university as "a place where the universality of the human spirit manifests itself" and where, because "science and investigation recognize as their aim the truth only … institutions which serve the interests of science [such as universities, of course; ALO/GSD] should be a factor making for a union of nations and men". Lamenting and admonishing the rise of antisemitism and nationalism in European universities, he continued in "the hope that our University will always be free from this evil, that teachers and students will preserve the consciousness that they serve people best when they maintain its union with humanity and with the highest human values". At the same time, Einstein prescribed the goals of "our" Hebrew University so that they specifically address the needs of the Jewish people and of the Zionist society establishing itself in Palestine at that time. First, while hoping that "one of their noblest tasks [is] to keep our people free from nationalistic obscurantism and aggressive intolerance", he also recognized that "Jewish nationalism is today a necessity because only through a consolidation of our national life can we eliminate those conflicts from which the Jews suffer today". Likewise, second, he juxtaposed worldliness alongside Jewish exceptionalism: while hoping that soon-after Jewish nationalism will be "thoroughly a matter of course" and Jews will be inspired "with assurance and pride vis-à-vis the entire world", Einstein also hoped that "this institution will demonstrate with the greatest clearness the achievements of which the Jewish spirit is capable". Also, the last set of Einstein's hopes for "our university" was specific to the Jewry world and the Zionist Jewish settlers: in this open letter, he specified that "a special task devolves upon the University in the spiritual direction and education of the labouring sections of our people in the land", noting that "we aim at creating a people of workers", thus rallying to the Zionist call to create a new Jew, breaking away from religious orthodoxy and Shteitl lives of Diasporic Jewry. Also, specifically addressing the Zionist Jewish settlers, Einstein declared the special missions devolving upon the university, in addition to education and spiritual direction: "to create something unique in order to serve the specific needs of the forms of life developed by our people in Palestine". In this way, the Hebrew University, he hoped, would become a "spiritual center" whose achievements will not only "penetrate" – meaning impress and sway – "the large masses of Jewry" but also "evoke the respect of cultured mankind the world over". Still, as much as Einstein was explicit in his address of Jewish and Zionist issues of the time (Gutfreund, 2008), the appeal is also universal in its address of the university's humanistic social role.

Einstein's open letter of 1925 stands as a manifesto for the relations between academia and society: as much as it was about Jewish and Zionist particularities, it also set parameters for how the university is a "lighthouse" for, rather than an "ivory tower" set apart from, human society. Much like Einstein stands as an iconic figure for science and humanity (see Galison et al., 2008), so stands his 1925 proclamation as a beacon for setting university–society relations. Furthermore, this proclamation's brevity stems exactly from its demand that the university is to be defined through its relations with, and impact on, the concentric communities and societies in which it is embedded.

Nowadays, the practice of universities composing a mission statement is commonplace worldwide. The practice is often prescribed as a compulsory part of current-day strategic exercises at universities, following the Ashridge Model of vision–mission–goals (see Campbell and Yeung, 1991). The mission statements of universities today are highly isomorphic in content and style, mostly due to their shared reliance on a cadre of professionalized experts (Drori, 2016). As mentioned earlier, many of these principles are at the core of the *Magna Charta Universitatum*, which was issued and ratified by 388 university rectors and residents from Europe and beyond in September 1988 in Bologna, and since then it has expanded its base of ratification to 889 universities from 88 countries (in 2018) and created the basis for the European Higher Education Area (EHEA). This Bologna proclamation calls on universities "to play [a role] in a changing and increasingly international society", to stand as "true universities" (i.e., as "centres of culture, knowledge and research"), to uphold "the future of mankind that is dependent on cultural, scientific and technical developments", and to educate and train future generations. Yet, alongside such inspiring calls, much of the Bologna Proclamation is devoted to protecting university autonomy, "morally and intellectually independent from political authority and economic power". Therefore, the Bologna proclamation is mostly concerned with the two important academic principles of academic freedom and institutional autonomy, at the expense of boldly expressing a commitment to social relevance, social involvement, and social impact. In addition, this proclamation too is steeped in the formula of the Ashridge Model for mission–vision–goals and in the standards of UN conventions, thus moving from the Preamble statement to Principles to Means. Overall, these various current-day efforts to inspire, articulate, and specify the course of university–society relations by composing a mission statement, because of their standardized form and their focus on deliverables, pale in comparison with the scope and brevity of Einstein's 1925 open letter.

## BOX 4.3 THE MAGNA CHARTA UNIVERSITATUM

**Preamble**

The undersigned Rectors of European Universities, gathered in Bologna for the ninth centenary of the oldest University in Europe, four years before the definitive abolition of boundaries between the countries of the European Community; looking forward to far-reaching co-operation between all European nations and believing that people and States should become more than ever aware of the part that universities will be called upon to play in a changing and increasingly international society,

**Consider**

1. that at the approaching end of this millennium the future of mankind depends largely on cultural, scientific and technical development; and that this is built up in centres of culture, knowledge and research as represented by true universities;
2. that the universities' task of spreading knowledge among the younger generations implies that, in today's world, they must also serve society as a whole; and that the cultural, social and

economic future of society requires, in particular, a considerable investment in continuing education;
3. that universities must give future generations education and training that will teach them, and through them others, to respect the great harmonies of their natural environment and of life itself.

The undersigned Rectors of European universities proclaim to all States and to the conscience of all nations the fundamental principles, which must, now and always, support the vocation of universities.

**Fundamental principles**

1. The university is an autonomous institution at the heart of societies differently organised because of geography and historical heritage; it produces, examines, appraises and hands down culture by research and teaching. To meet the needs of the world around it, its research and teaching must be morally and intellectually independent of all political authority and economic power.
2. Teaching and research in universities must be inseparable if their tuition is not to lag behind changing needs, the demands of society, and advances in scientific knowledge.
3. Freedom in research and training is the fundamental principle of university life, and governments and universities, each as far as in them lies, must ensure respect for this fundamental requirement. Rejecting intolerance and always open to dialogue, a university is an ideal meeting-ground for teachers capable of imparting their knowledge and well equipped to develop it by research and innovation and for students entitled, able and willing to enrich their minds with that knowledge.
4. A university is the trustee of the European humanist tradition; its constant care is to attain universal knowledge; to fulfil its vocation it transcends geographical and political frontiers, and affirms the vital need for different cultures to know and influence each other.

**The means**

To attain these goals by following such principles calls for effective means, suitable to present conditions.

> 1. To preserve freedom in research and teaching, the instruments appropriate to realise that freedom must be made available to all members of the university community.
> 2. Recruitment of teachers, and regulation of their status, must obey the principle that research is inseparable from teaching.
> 3. Each university must – with due allowance for particular circumstances – ensure that its students' freedoms are safeguarded, and that they enjoy concessions in which they can acquire the culture and training which it is their purpose to possess.
> 4. Universities – particularly in Europe – regard the mutual exchange of information and documentation, and frequent joint projects for the advancement of learning, as essential to the steady progress of knowledge.
>
> Therefore, as in the earliest years of their history, they encourage mobility among teachers and students; furthermore, they consider a general policy of equivalent status, titles, examinations (without prejudice to national diplomas) and award of scholarships essential to the fulfilment of their mission in the conditions prevailing today.
>
> The undersigned Rectors, on behalf of their Universities, undertake to do everything in their power to encourage each State, as well as the supranational organisations concerned, to mould this policy sedulously on this Magna Charta, which expresses the universities' unanimous desire freely determined and declared.
>
> Bologna, 18 September 1988

**Einstein as a Role Model for ACL**

From these three tales, we can draw a few lessons. First, it is easier for renowned scientists to exchange their capital for social impact; in doing so, they signify the importance of leadership and a strong normative stand of social justice, social integration, and equality; care for the public good and well-being; and integrating science and social responsibility. This does not exclude other academicians from drawing on ACL principles to encourage bottom-up leadership. They can still use their academic, social, and symbolic capital to leverage ACL activities. Second, a scientist does not necessarily need to be an expert in every social area in order to act with the conception of ACL. Human values and social norms can guide any scientist in identifying areas such as injustice and equal rights.

## INTEGRATION: ACL AS PATHWAYS FOR ADVANCEMENT AND PROTECTION OF THE PUBLIC GOOD

The expansive review of ACL and ACL-themed practices that we offer here describes the already existing academic practices alongside newly initiated practices. Seeing the long history of university–society relations, do these practices and the ACL strategy redefine the university? In the following section, we propose three categories of the social roles of universities, each charting a pathway by which universities advance and protect the public good. These three social role categories are not necessarily exhaustive or mutually exclusive. Nevertheless, they provide an analytic backbone for the classification of ACL exemplars (see section "Contemporary Varieties, with a Long History", earlier in Chapter 4), which superimposes ACL onto the types of social engagements typical of the classic university missions. The following three pathways respond to the question, what is the role of universities building the capacity for academic commitment and leadership? This review suggests that through such practices, academicians and universities alike activate their commitment and leadership as a new form of defining their social role.

**1. Universities as social integrators**

Once universities are committed to opening their gates, they bring together students from a greater range of social strata, with highly diverse backgrounds and from across the boundaries of gender, ethnicity, citizenship, economic status and income levels, political preferences, parents' occupations, and general interest. While students from such diverse backgrounds come together in their classes, according to their disciplinary preferences, they become exposed to those representing socially remote groups and learn to engage with people different than them.

This is not to claim that such exposure does not take place under other circumstances – for example, in integrated elementary and high schools, the military, or other social situations where diversity is encouraged or institutionalized. Nevertheless, with academic education requiring students to step outside their native region, either nationally or internationally, academia increasingly becomes a uniquely important site for countering social segregation and advancing social integration. In this regard, the task ahead of universities is to challenge the dynamics of social reproduction by dismantling hurdles set before first-generation students and countering the dynamics of social closure by establishing diversity. Specific to ACL, the university's role as a site for social integrators enables the definition of the public good: it expands to dimensions of "the public" through familiarity with a more diverse set of social groups, and it strives to wrestle, in such diverse company, with the definition of such social "good".

## 2. Universities as a greenhouse of social leadership by mentoring, expectation setting, and socialization

The intellectual elite have long been defined by their ability to acquire advanced education, and this includes the status group of the educated who became the service class of the regime. In this regard, universities have long been the hothouses for the elite – alternatively described as the intelligentsia, the "new class" of state bureaucracy, or specifically the professional elite. While some of the university's role in this regard has been in the training of the elite (a task that is still associated with, for example, the French *grandes écoles*), universities are increasingly open to broader social strata. In this capacity, universities serve as systems for "expectation-setting" and as sites for socialization, thus propagating modes of rationalized and critical thinking and enculturating into universalistic values of world society.

As sites for expectation-setting, universities drive the particular definition of the "ideal citizen", constituted around themes of mastery, self-driven innovation, aspiration for excellence, and orientation towards action. These features of personhood are nowadays the threshold for admissions to universities, features of higher education, and criteria for promotion in academia.

In these various roles, universities redefine the public good to which they are committing themselves. Specifically, ACL departs from the form of academia–society relations prized to date by adding an explicit focus on social impact and social import. Therefore, in addition to their role as training centres for the elite, they provide their students with observational and analytical tools. The ability to observe and analyse ideas or data and allow for alternative thinking or models of explanations is an important capability and resource. With such capabilities, it is possible to reflect on alternative options for social policy or social action, to analyse the value and costs of such alternatives, both economically and socially, and to make well-thought-out and reviewed decisions.

On this front, universities and university scholars can contribute to actions of social responsibility: experts of policy analysis can offer careful policy options in areas where social change is needed; economists have the capability to contribute to the analysis of possible national budget allocations and their impact on social processes and needed change; health experts can offer better programmes to assist in public health education as well as the improvement of public health systems; and education experts can develop more effective teaching methods and systems that will contribute to a wider success rate in teaching various subjects.

Critical thinking capabilities are valuable resources since they provide better tools to develop and evaluate change-based capabilities and understanding. Such critical thinking can also convince governmental agencies and policymakers in need to make changes in certain social areas or even act as "eye openers" in different social fronts in cases where the causes and effects of social problems were not detected.

In Israel, for example, many scholars from the area of economics, education, social work, and social policy are participating in public debates on issues of government policies or in areas where there are plans with regards to social change. Critical and noncritical research findings are shared with the public, government agencies, and policymakers, and these become a part of the decision-making process on such issues. This is, of course, not a practice that is unique to Israel, and in many countries, we can see evidence where the capabilities associated with critical thinking were shared with the public.

In the search for excellence and high achievements, coupled with the front of gaining knowledge, universities are an arena for expectation-setting. In stating this, we mean that universities have the ability to draw students towards ACL activities. Such expectation-setting processes can be targeted towards issues of social leadership and responsibility. Examples of such processes can include the actions taken by law students to act in a community setting for the benefit of those who are at a disadvantage and in need of community activities, or medical students who reach out to those who suffer from medical problems but do not have the resources or ability to seek proper health treatment to ease their health problems.

Expectations that are set by universities, faculties, or departments towards areas of activities that capture social responsibly and leadership can bring about valuable social change. Such activities can be voluntary and encourage students and faculty to participate as a part of their commitment towards the public good. It is also possible to assign credit points or offer action-oriented classes where applied practices are expected so that the students benefit from the applied learning and so that stakeholders who are in need in the community benefit as well.

Universities are also hothouses for responsible social change leaders. In recent years, we have witnessed universities developing special classes for "social entrepreneurship", "community activities", or "leadership and responsibility" as some examples. Such classes are based on expectations that seem to emerge bottom-up from the students and top-down by some university professors or departments to establish a new entrepreneurial area of teaching and practice – that is, social entrepreneurship.

One example is Ashoka, a worldwide organization that focuses on social entrepreneurship, which has a unit that focuses on universities titled Ashoka U.[6] The aim of Ashoka U was to establish a consortium that would grow to 30 campuses by 2015. The goal stated by Askoka U was expressed as the following: "After establishing an institutional partnership with select universities, Ashoka works with teams of entrepreneurial students and faculty to accelerate their growth as hubs of social innovation".[7] The activities of Ashoka worldwide added significantly to the creation of a culture of social entrepreneurship within universities.

Intellectual leaders and scientific scholars establish their prominence and reputation while working in universities – teaching, conducting research, and publishing their ideas, findings, and scholarly work. Establishing academic reputation places the university scholar in the public eye and, as a result, endows her or him with the opportunity to act as an academic leader. Such leadership is valuable within the scientific field of the scholar and within the university as it offers the ability to direct the community (whether the scientific community in the scholar's field or the university community with which the scholar is affiliated) to issues of value and need for change. Einstein's role in public affairs is an obvious example, but there are many other, albeit less dramatic, examples of academics making use of their reputation and public visibility to advocate for, and lead action, towards social change.

However, a major change that can have the highest impact on the community at large is when an academic leader, who gained a high level of reputation with the scientific and general public, directs his or her activities towards creating some value changes in society or leading large projects of social change. This is when their reputation is so well established that the media and the public are interested in hearing and echoing their messages and are willing to follow them in the creation of change. Such valuable power is, although rare, an ultimate resource for social change, and academic responsible leadership has a greater likelihood of creating a social impact. The example of Einstein as a social leader who took initiatives in establishing a clear voice on social issues is most illuminating. His high level of symbolic capital in the nature of prestige and his scientific authority (Bourdieu and Wacquant, 2013) were instrumental in forming connections between scientists, scholars, and social activists, as well as in establishing a social impact on various social arenas, as presented in the three tales.

### 3. Universities as institutions generating diffusion spillover

As social institutions, universities facilitate the establishment of norms and generate expectations of high-level qualities as their intended outcome. If this is indeed the case, the established agglomeration of values and quality has the ability to diffuse to the social environment, thus generating spillover that can lead to positive, responsible outcomes. Biligi University in Istanbul is noted as an exemplary case (see Dahan and Senol, 2012). This private university was established by a social activist, and, upon founding, it adopted the principle of learning "not for school but for life". The university has a few campuses located in the low-income areas of Istanbul. Some faculty members with whom I talked told me that one of the goals of establishing the campuses in these areas was to achieve additional social goals. The campus classes and facilities became open to the youth of the neighbourhood a few times during the year in order to provide them with academic experience and to expose them to the possibilities of academic learning. Also, scholars from the university could go out to the nearby community and give lectures at schools and in public places.

The diffusion, or spillover, of ACL practices can thus be achieved when universities open their boundaries (either physical or metaphorical) to the general public or to specific parts of the public and share with them the wealth of research they possess in order to diffuse norms and facilitate social change. The campuses can become open to the public by inviting people to enjoy the facilities, such as libraries, public lectures, scientific camps for youth, major laboratories or special archives, and so on.

Of course, the diffusion can also be achieved when university scholars and students act in the community. Such activities can be in schools, exposing school-level students to academic research, and in public places in the community. For example, the Hebrew University has a day every year where its leading scientists give talks in pubs, museums, their own homes, or other public places. These talks are open to all communities in Jerusalem and are attended by many participants. The public message in these activities is that the university is a member of the community and has an interest in participating and sharing ideas and resources with the community. Such talks can attract more community members to enrol in formal learning or further explore their areas of interest.

Obviously, speaking in the media can generate paths for the diffusion of ideas and norms. Academic scholars are invited to give their opinion or analysis of many issues that are of great interest to the public. Such exposure to the general community can become a valuable source for diffusing values and facilitating activities of social responsibility in various areas.

## SUMMARY: MANY TYPES, ONE MISSION

In this chapter, we offered an overview of the history leading up to the contemporary university and showed how universities contribute to the public good. We showed how universities have added to the advancement of the public good and social issues, allowing for a broad spectrum of targets and courses. Further, we aimed to illustrate some examples of academic leadership and social activism. We described cases of academic leadership aiming for social impact and change and driven by both academicians and scientists as mainly bottom-up processes of responsibility and action. Finally, we characterized three main pathways and example strategies of universities with regards to ACL. These refer to universities as social integrators, a greenhouse of social leadership by mentoring, expectation-setting, and socialization, and institutions generating diffusion spillover. These three pathways have become institutionalizing structures and practices that encourage ACL and socialize new entrants into such a culture, while also pertaining to the three existing missions of academia.

Through our discussion of exemplary ACL practices, illustration of examples of bottom-up leadership and activism, and characterization of the three main pathways of universities, we show that there are many types and directions. However, they are all integrated under the umbrella of one new mission.

> At the approaching end of this millennium the future of mankind depends largely on cultural, scientific and technical development; and, ... this is built up in centers of culture, knowledge and research represented by true universities. (Preamble, *Magna Charta Universitatum* (Bologna Declaration), September 1988)

## NOTES

1. See *Times Higher Education*'s SDG-specific rankings of universities at www.thewur.com or #THEglobalimact.
2. Einstein's Archives, Box 36, file 28-529, 1–2. Reproduced courtesy of the Albert Einstein Archives, The Hebrew University of Jerusalem, Israel, and Princeton University Press.
3. Einstein Archives, file 57-543. Reproduced courtesy of the Albert Einstein Archives, The Hebrew University of Jerusalem, Israel, and Princeton University Press.
4. See Box 4.1. Source: https://pugwash.org/1955/07/09/statement-manifesto, accessed 16 November 2019.
5. Source: https://www.wiseinternational.org/nuclear-monitor/802/albert-einstein-nuclear-weapon.
6. Source: https://www.ashoka.org/changemakercampus.
7. Source: Ashoka website https://www.babson.edu/academics/centers-and-institutes/the-lewis-institute/ashoka-u/#.

# 5. The Hoffman Leadership and Responsibility Programme at the Hebrew University: exemplar ACL community of practice within a university

Some activities of academic commitment and leadership (ACL) must be facilitated through membership in a community of "likeminded" academicians (e.g., community of practice) whose members express interest in commitment to the fourth mission of the university. To recap, this mission is about establishing socially related activities and taking a leadership role within them. The main question in this context is what the nature of such a community should be, how it should operate, what its missions should be, what the normative basis of such a community should be, and who should be included in the activities.

In this chapter, we focus on the issue of establishing and facilitating a cohesive and meaningful "community of practice" from a group of unrelated and highly diverse doctoral students. Such an ongoing group was established at the Hebrew University and has been operating for 14 years. We will describe it in more detail later on, and we outline here the main elements that became the founding ideas that facilitated the programme's development. These ideas are borrowed from chaos theory and include "bottom-up" and "top-down" processes of group-formation practices, processes developing self-organizing teams, and empowerment practices, and they facilitate self-reflection and critical thinking. All of these processes are related to the group culture that emerged. Further, in this chapter, we review and discuss the contents and main themes selected for the meetings and describe then in some detail based on notes taken during the many meetings.

## "COMMUNITIES OF PRACTICE"

The concept of a community of practice is an important building infrastructure, both symbolically and practically, for establishing strong ACL. As an organizational phenomenon and practice, this concept was developed by several scholars in various disciplines using somewhat different angles (e.g., Duguid, 2005; Wenger and Snyder, 2000).

For the purpose of our discussion in this book, we would like to elaborate on the concept suggested by Wenger (2010) and introduce the major building blocks he suggested. In this general outline of communities and social learning, Wenger described communities of practice as the form of social gathering where people share cultural practices and reflect on their collective learning. Participation in these communities is essential for social learning and leads to meaningful knowing. Communities of practice are the "social containers" of the competences that make up a social system. These communities define competences by combining three elements:

1. Members are bound together by their collective understanding of the meaning of their community, and together they generate a sense of "joint enterprise".
2. The community is built through mutual engagement. Through internal interactions, norms of mutual understanding are established, and there is a sense of "mutuality". Competence is now defined as being a member of the community and being trusted in the community's interactions.
3. Within communities of practice, a "shared repertoire" of communal resources is developed, and this includes language, routines, artefacts, tools, stories, style, norms, and so on. Competence now also includes the ability to access these repertoires and use them in an appropriate way.

The growth of such communities is enabled through the "convergent interplay of competence and experience that involve mutual engagement" (Wenger, 2000, p. 229). In the process, there are opportunities to negotiate competence through experience that results from direct mutual participation. Thus, such communities remain important processes that establish social units of learning. The learning can be diffused to larger communities and become a central part of a much larger constellation of other interrelated communities of practice.

The dimensions that facilitate progress in such communities are *enterprise*, *mutuality*, and *repertoire*. We describe these three dimensions of Wenger (2000) in the following manner. First, the concept of enterprise refers to the level of learning energy. It asks about the degree to which the community takes initiative in keeping and maintaining learning as a core activity. For this goal, the community needs to show leadership in pushing its development along a spirit of exploration and inquiry. The learning energy should encompass both the gaps in knowledge and understanding as well as the openness to new directions of exploration and creative thinking where new ideas can flourish.

Second, the concept of mutuality is about capturing the depth of the social capital established jointly by group members. The process of interactions within the group should aim to deepen the sense of mutual engagement over time. First, group members need to know each other well to a degree that permits interactions for seeking advice and support for their activities. The interactions should lead to a deep sense of trust in other members both in terms of accepting their advice and assistance and sharing with them openly positive and negative aspects of their own activities. Only such a level of closeness and strong mutuality will allow group members to feel comfortable in addressing core issues of their activities and to feel rewarded by giving and receiving assistance from their peers. With such mutual contributions, the group can learn about the richness of various members' qualities and capabilities and benefit from exposure to them.

Finally, the concept of repertoire refers to the degree of self-awareness. This element focuses on internal processes of group members in which they become conscious about the community and repertoire they develop. Within the community of practice, meaning is negotiated through the shared repertoire. The shared repertoire becomes a pool of resources that community members contribute to, and this leads to the renewal of the community. In addition, such awareness includes understanding the effects of the repertoire in practice, understanding the concepts and language used by the group, and developing group tools for establishing their perspective on the world.

The ability of the group to be reflective on its repertoire and practices enables its members to learn about the core assumptions, perspectives, and practices they share. Self-awareness is an important tool that allows the group to progress and evolve into a meaningful community of practice.

To design a meaningful community of practice, Wenger (2000) suggested that there is a need for a few components that create cohesion and bonding within the group and that generate the needed resources to maintain and further develop the group's activities as a community. In the next section, we present the main components and describe how they were manifested in the Hoffman programme. The components include the following:

**a. Public events**

Community-based public events bring members of the community together. If these events are attentive to the needs of the community, they will add to its mission and sense of purpose. A community becomes organic when the members design the events in which they wish to participate in terms of the types of activities they feel are essential to achieving their goals. Such public events can be formal or informal, with external guest speakers, sessions on joint problem-solving, or sessions on developing capabilities and understanding of alternative routines or practices.

In accordance with this principle,

- Hoffman fellows met every other week in a campus facility designed to meet their needs. Each meeting lasted four hours, and the fellows were those responsible for choosing the topics to be discussed, inviting the speakers, and organizing and managing the meeting sessions. Numerous breaks between the various sessions in each meeting allowed the fellows to continue their informal conversations over snacks and coffee.
- Hoffman fellows received the programme and the timetable a week in advance. This was usually accompanied by reading materials on the topics introduced in the main speaker's lecture or in the topic of discussion. The readings enhanced awareness and initial thoughts on the topics.
- Attendance at the meetings of the Hoffman programme was mandatory and set as a fixed requirement in the fellowship contract. However, the norm was that fellows were allowed to miss a couple of meetings throughout the year due to other activities, illness, or travel. There was only one occasion when we had to deal with frequent non-attendance, and this was when a fellow was trying to raise funding for the NGO he established while serving as a fellow in the

programme. We were impressed to see that the level of commitment to group activities was extremely high, to the degree that fellows arrived (1) after a long flight on two occasions; (2) a couple of weeks after delivering a baby; (3) while feeling ill; or (4) with sick children (we allowed mothers and fathers to bring their children and babies if they needed to, and we allowed them to sit off to the side and play or read. Usually, such visits did not interfere with the group activities). Nursing mothers were encouraged to bring their babies as long as they felt they needed to and to move in and out of the room as they needed. This too was never a problem. In one case, we had a baby with us for 14 months, and only when the baby started to talk and cheerfully "contributed" to the discussion did her mother leave her with a babysitter.

### b. Leadership

Communities of practice need to establish internal leadership that will assist the community in its development. A formal community coordinator is required who will receive information from members and disseminate the needed information on group members and activities to the community. However, in addition, there is a need to establish group leaders who can operate in different capacities – that is, plan meetings, generate network contacts for community members, and share information on resource availability. Others can document group practices, contact public speakers, or facilitate groups' informal activities or subgroups' informal meetings. These leadership activities are both a resource for the group and role models of leadership activities and practices.

In accordance with this principle,

- The Hoffman programme was about taking a leadership position in expressing social responsibility roles and actions. The fact that the fellows were chosen based on their leadership qualities created a challenge. It was difficult to facilitate a programme where everyone was encouraged to take leadership-related actions and responsibilities. After all, in most social groups, the number of leaders is smaller than the number of group members. However, the internal variety of group members' characteristics made this "multiple leadership challenge" a smooth process due to a few reasons. First, we developed the conception of multiple role models for leadership qualities. All

fellows operated under the expectation that they were to be active within the group throughout the various activities and contribute as a role model for the others. Within the group activities, members were equally valued and had shared and joint contributions, and outside of the group, they were taking leadership initiatives within their various activities and social circles. Thus, the internal community of practice was also about sharing resources and role models on leadership capabilities and qualities, allowing each member to take a leading responsibility on some of the group activities by assigned tasks.
- Nevertheless, even among such a selective group of fellows with leadership qualities, some became more prominent than others and were involved more actively in the group's planning and discussions. In addition, as the programme was characterized by many sets of decisions, some fellows had a stronger influence on how to plan the next activities, what topics should be discussed, which speakers should be invited, and so on. It is of interest to note that due to the egalitarian culture of the group, the democratic decision-making process, and the close friendships that evolved between the fellows, there was not even one incident where such processes were associated with expressed conflicts. The group always accepted the initiatives of the internal leaders as an acknowledgement of their expertise. For example, when one group member, who is an expert in NGOs on gender empowerment, suggested sites for group visits, her suggestion was accepted upfront. When another member, who is a geography doctoral student, suggested a field trip for the group, his proposal was accepted by all group members.

### c. Connectivity

Group meetings can become a valuable vehicle for the mobilization of joint interests or activities if they generate internal group cohesion. The opportunities for group members to engage in meaningful conversations and exchanges may lead to further joint activities, and valuable exchanges become a natural outcome of well-connected groups that share strong norms and interests. In the era of multiple interactive media platforms, it is of value to develop alternative forms where the community members can interact.

In accordance with this principle,

- It was always an important goal for us at the programme to try to create the needed group culture and atmosphere that would facilitate group cohesion. However, this was a difficult goal to achieve, especially when the group was composed of such a wide range of characteristics of the various fellows as well as their constraints and interests. Over the years, we noticed that there are several mechanisms that can enhance cohesion for such a diverse group. First, we allowed for relatively long periods of informal time so that fellows could socialize and become familiar with each other's thoughts and ideas. If such breaks between sessions are facilitated by a flexible space where people can sit and stand, be in a quiet zone, or be in a crowded public space, supplemented with refreshments, stronger group cohesion emerges.
- Breaking into small discussion groups is a most valuable mechanism as well. In contrast to the activities that took place in the large group of 36 fellows, in the small discussion groups, every group member had an opportunity to express his or her opinion and hear the opinion of other members. Forming different groups in various sessions (while switching between group members) generates an opportunity for each group member to get to know, over a set of sessions, all the members of the community. It is of great value to alternate between discussions within the whole community and the small discussion groups. After the small group discussions, we returned to the whole community so that each group could deliver the key ideas. For small discussion groups that took longer than 5–10 minutes, we established the practice of moving out of the meeting room to external informal areas or changing the seating so that the small groups were seated around smaller tables in various places of the meeting space.
- We also held some special sessions with a different format – we titled them "unconferences". These were "surprise and unorganized sessions". Once or twice a year, we announced a four-hour unconference session. Every fellow prepared a mini-lecture or presentation on any topic he or she wanted to share or discuss. The mini-lectures were around 15 to 20 minutes. The titles of the sessions were placed on a board in the morning. There were three parallel sessions, and every participant could move between the sessions as they wished. Every hour, we had a small break that allowed for informal discussions, grouping, and regrouping. These unconference days were exciting. The fellows learned more about each other, new interest groups were formed, and a wide range of learning took place. The openness and

flexibility of such sessions greatly enhanced connectivity within the group and the appreciation fellows felt towards each other and the programme.
- The design of the convening room for such community of practice work is important. We built the central table as a composition of eight smaller tables. The main room was designed so that all 36 group members were seated around the large centre table during the presentations, talks, and formal discussions. When smaller discussions were needed, the eight tables could be pulled apart, and informal groups could gather around them, which allowed for greater flexibility in the group practices. These smaller tables could also be used at other times, during other types of gatherings (such as our meeting with the families of our donors), so that food could be served or materials could be displayed on the tables.

**d. Membership**

A vibrant and productive community needs a critical mass of members (Oliver and Montgomery, 2008). A critical mass will contribute to the generation of a cohesive group of practices. Once there is a sufficient number of members in a community of practice, the activities can generate solidarity and legitimacy for the group practices and goals. To maintain a cohesive group, it is important to create socializing processes for new group members. Effective transition and socialization, from being new to the group to becoming a fully committed community member, will result in members' continued enthusiasm in the activities and practices of the community.

In accordance with this principle:

- The first year of the programme was designed to have twelve fellows. This group's size was certainly too small for establishing a community of practice. In cases where two members were missing, the group felt too small, and when any member came a bit late or had to leave early, it caused disruption to the group processes. During the second year, an additional 12 fellows joined the group. This group size required a larger room, but almost every seminar room on campus was well suited for a group of 24 members. The third year of the programme was designed to have 36 fellows, and this has been the steady state size of the group since then.

- A community of 36 fellows generated new dynamics. On the one hand, constraints were associated with each member not having sufficient time to talk during the sessions. In addition, there were hardly any seminar rooms on campus that could properly accommodate such a group with all fellows seated around the large table. This seating arrangement is a critical element characterizing the egalitarian nature of the group as well as the face-to-face eye contact needed for such a community, especially during complex discussions.

e. **Learning projects**

A meaningful learning agenda and projects are important for deepening the commitment to the community of practice activities. Community members need to take responsibility for initiating and planning meaningful learning events, projects, and activities that define and fill gaps in the actions, knowledge, and understanding of the community of practice. Such gaps may include assessing practice-related tools, developing needed capabilities, and building a mutual design of a project, including specifying goals and challenges, establishing contact with academic research projects in areas related to the community activities and interests, and so on.

In accordance with this principle,

- The group's learning practices each year were based on the decisions made by the group members. Each year we had a general topic, and the fellows suggested specific topics they were motivated to cover. We believed that it was of great value to establish the routine in which group members were responsible for deciding what they wished to learn and who they wished to invite as speakers or mentors for the group. This way, a strong sense of group-level self-efficacy was established, and the learning was based on a combination of individual and group motivations. In this context, one year the group members expressed a wish to have more internal discussions on their own projects of volunteering and social responsibility rather than inviting external speakers. After the group discussion on this need, members decided that a few sessions would be designed and designated for such internal learning processes during the following semester. Group members who were in charge of these meetings had to decide how to best arrange these sessions, which included the following questions: Who will be selected to speak? How many of the group members will speak? How much time will be given to each speaker? What will be the length of the Q&A period? How many parallel speakers will there be? and so on.

**f.   Artefacts**

The role of community-related artefacts should not be ignored. Relevant artefacts include stories, symbols, tools, documents, and titles for community activities. The energy and resources needed for establishing the community artefacts need to come from members of the community and their leaders. The continuous reference and use of the artefacts maintain their legitimacy and value of meaning for the community of practice.

In accordance with this principle,

– Important artefacts for our group included a logo of the group, designed by the group members; a group t-shirt; designed nametags for all group members so they would know each other by name; and more. We also assigned formal and fun titles for each activity. For example, a discussion took place once a year after the feedback reports that were based on the first semester activities, and there was an open session titled "home improvement". In this session, group members expressed their desires for changes in some of the group activities, time arrangements, or topics they wished to cover. Another title was given to the second part of each session where a new group member told the group a short narrative about him- or herself with no structuring or specific guidelines. This part took about ten minutes and was titled "personal statement".
– The programme had a website and a Facebook account where all of the fellows' background and contact information were available. On the website, we posted additional information on the group meetings and activities as well as photos of the group activities and fellows.

## BUILDING ACL ON COMMUNITIES OF PRACTICE AND GROUP BOUNDARIES

In our view, group boundaries are valuable for establishing meaningful communities of practice. They are important for generating community-based learning, and they are also building blocks for community power and empowered group membership.

In his thoughtful essay, Wenger (2000) discussed the importance of understanding the group boundaries and their contribution to the processes taken by the community of practice. In Wenger's paradigmatic conceptualization of communities of practice, boundaries are important for learning systems because they connect communities and offer learning opportunities. He argued that learning inside a community takes place due to the convergence of competencies and experience and that this in turn allows a community to exist. Interactions within the group with clear membership boundaries allow members to expose their competences and experiences to others who have different competences, as well as establish configurations of relations between competence and experience into a meaningful learning experience. The notion of these configurations is the exposure to challenges that represent tensions between certain competences and experiences, and these are the source for learning.

The learning within the group's boundaries is at its best when the community and individuals within it can observe tensions between competence and experience, and such gaps lead to a strong need to share and learn within the community. Four main features are required to gain meaningful learning within the community. I will specify them using Wenger's terms and further elaborate on them. The four features include the following:

- Something to interact about – sharing interests, attending interesting talks, and participating in challenging discussions are the basic building blocks for establishing meaningful interactions.
- Open engagement with others on real differences and on common grounds – for achieving such different/common discussions, the multifaceted heterogeneity of group members, interest, and experience is important. The heterogeneity of members and the differences between them are needed for establishing a meaningful learning experience within the community boundaries. Obviously, there is also a need for common ground in order to start the interest and motivation for interactions. The common ground in our case was the commitment for taking social responsibility and acting upon it.
- Commitment of suspending judgement on competence – if judgment by group members is articulated at early stages and critical comments are expressed, learning will be halted, and no real experience will be shared. Therefore, it is important that community members express

the commitment to hold judgement and allow for free sharing of experiences and competences between group members so as to facilitate community-based learning.
- Means for "translating" repertoires that allow for competence and experience to interact – as the diversity between the characteristics, interests, competences, and experiences is wide, it is important to understand that translating the repertoires expressed to other group members is not a simple process. Such translations require further discussions about meanings and reasons, where group members can freely express questions and comments while trying to understand the "deep experience" that is described by group members.

As argued by Wenger (2000), group boundaries are not just important for meaningful learning. There are other dimensions to the importance of forming group boundaries for communities of practice. Forming such clear group boundaries is associated with exclusivity and group identity (Theiss-Morse, 2009) and establishing distinct and high requirements because entry to group activities can enhance the empowerment of group members and collective identity (Polletta and Jasper, 2001).

The discussion of the boundaries' importance was theorized and studied by Montgomery and Oliver (2007) and Oliver and Montgomery (2008) in the context of professional power. Their main argument was that "Understanding boundary-spanning activities such as interorganizational alliances and professional/organizational integration requires clarity about what boundaries are being spanned and how they were constructed" (Montgomery and Oliver, 2007, p. 661). Their approach to the issue of boundaries of social groups is based on social identity theory and institutional theory to develop a process model, whereby inward- and outward-directed networking activities combine to build the social boundaries marking exclusive membership and proprietary domain. Thus, the argument is that the strength of the boundaries and the exclusivity of the community are important features in the process of generating internal commitment and connectivity as well as establishing external legitimacy and influence to act within the society at large.

Identity is an important component in group learning. Wenger (2000) argued that "if knowing is an act of belonging, then our identities are a key structuring element of how we know" (p. 238). Developing an identity that is associated with the community is valuable for a few reasons. Identities are a combination of competence and experience that lead to a sense of knowing. These identities become the key factor in deciding what is important, who to interact with, who can be trusted, and what we need to learn. Identities require an ability to be flexible during group interactions. Opening individual identities to the shared interactions with other group members is associated with group learning. It is also important to note that identities are the connecting bridges between communities. Through sharing personal identities that are related to other communities of membership, bridges across communities are established. This is how new knowledge and learning can be synergized with internal group activities.

Progress in integrating different identities of group members into the practices of the community is gained through three mechanisms (Wenger, 2000, p. 239): connectedness, expansiveness, and effectiveness.

## NETWORKS OF PRACTICE

Duguid (2005) introduced some related concepts to communities of practice, such as "networks of practice" that are not based necessarily on face-to-face interactions and are not necessarily geographically localized. These networks are based on practices that are shared widely among practitioners, even if they have never contacted or met each other. Such networks include all practitioners of a specific practice. An example is the "epistemic culture" concept developed by Knorr-Cetina (2009), who suggested that high-energy physicists constitute a global network of practice. Some are members of a community of practice, but they can also be members of the network of practice without meeting other members of the community face to face.

The core characteristics composing the networks are the fact that they share common tools and practices and that these can be exchanged from a distance and are based on "knowing that" and "knowing how" (Gherardi, 2011), which are both practice-based activities. Duguid (2005) distinguished between leaky and sticky knowledge in such networks and suggested that "where practice precedes it, explicit knowledge may appear to have global reach (or to be 'leaky'). Where it does not, the same knowledge may appear remarkably parochial (or to be 'sticky')" (p. 153). Thus, for knowledge to be leaky and have an extended reach, it is important that it follows meaningful practices for the individuals involved in the community.

Duguid (2005) further discussed the difference between community of practice and network of practice and claimed that the major difference is the control and coordination of the reproduction of a group and its practice. The new members to the community enter the network through a specific, reputable local community. Since, in communities of practice, the importance of tacit knowledge in the local community is high, the community shapes the identity of a newcomer and his or her trajectory. This does not happen as strongly in networks of practice, where the lack of face-to-face interactions between all members reduces that ability to transfer tacit knowledge and thus contributes strongly to the construction of community-related identity.

## EPISTEMIC AND ETHICAL ASPECTS OF PRACTICE

As the key element of communities of practice is the exchange of tacit knowledge between likeminded individuals, this practice has the ability to reduce the hardships in knowledge exchange. The institutional economic and sociological literature has argued that there are taxing effects of "transaction costs" in knowledge exchange (Williamson, 1981), hardships in access to information (Mokyr, 2002), and constraints resulting from the specification and protection of private interests (Oliver, 2004). In this context, the community of practice perspective reduces the effect of these assumptions of limiting information exchange along two distinct dimensions:

> On the one hand, there are difficulties around what knowledge people *can* meaningfully share. Such involuntary barriers to sharing might be thought of as epistemic entailments of practice. On the other, there are also difficulties concerning what people *will* share – not everything has its price. Local communities and even disaggregated networks of practice may simply not want to share, or they may want to hide what they know. (Duguid, 2005, p. 113)

The notions of "what can be shared" and "who will share" are two dimensions used in establishing a process of sharing. These need to be modified and flattened so that members within the community will openly share their insights and experiences. In addition, there is a need to establish the valuable contribution of the "knowing how" element of knowledge exchange in the exchanges within the community of practice. The concept of knowing how rather than "knowing what" changes the weight from focusing on knowledge to centring on experience, understanding, and insights. The value of the "knowing how" aspect is that it is connecting the epistemic ability of an actor to the experience and understanding aspects in the voluntary process of exchange and sharing.

## HOW DID WE FACILITATE GROUP COHESION AT THE HOFFMAN LEADERSHIP AND RESPONSIBILITY PROGRAMME?

In this section, we wish to offer a few illustrative examples for the practice of establishing learning communities of practice. These practices can add to the creation of group cohesion and social bonding as well as generate the needed resources to maintain and further develop the group's activities as a community.

However, before we start, there is a need to account for the constraining factors associated with the group and its special characteristics. There are various constraining factors associated with the establishment of a community of practice based on doctoral students who share activities related to their perceptions and activities of social responsibility and leadership, as it was in the Hoffman programme:

1. The programme fellows came from all of the academic disciplines, and, thus, there was a need to understand the differences associated with the wide range of disciplinary foci. The first difference regards the type of research in which they were involved – that is, some worked on a daily basis in a research laboratory and thus were not flexible with their time, whereas others spent most of their days in a library or archive and did not get a chance to talk with too many people during their working day. In addition, some fellows were involved in teaching and research, and others were working solely on research. In addition, research could be conducted all in one site or required travelling to various sites for data collection.

    The disciplinary background of the fellows was also associated with the degree of knowledge and the general understanding these doctoral students had with sociological, psychological, or political theories regarding social change, leadership, equality and stratification, social movements, social and human capital, and so on. Others had a great deal of knowledge and understanding of theories and research in these areas. Thus, this diversity of background theoretical knowledge had an impact on the general group discussions. For some fellows, issues regarding justice or equality were obvious and redundant, whereas such issues were new and enlightening for other members of the group.

2. The fellows had various personal constraints. As the group was always highly diverse, not only in terms of disciplinary background

but also in other background characteristics (including religion, religiosity level, ethnicity, gender, family composition etc.), it was difficult to plan group activities that could fit all group members and assure a high level of participation. For example, it was harder for the group members who had families and young children[1] to meet in the evenings or on weekends. Other examples included students who lived in the university dorms and returned home on weekends, thus limiting the meeting time options. In addition, those working in research laboratories had a lower level of flexibility in leaving their laboratory during the day for community activities.

3. The fellows were at different stages of their dissertation research. As some fellows entered the programme at the first year of their doctoral studies, others could enter at the beginning of the third year. In Israel, doctoral studies range between 4–8 years, and, thus, the 3-year fellowship did not cover the entire period of the doctoral programme. This variance leads to another – that is, the more advanced students were often busy working on publications, travelling to conferences, and searching for options for a postdoctoral programme. Thus, their mindset and attention were in a different place compared to the students who were at an early stage of their doctoral programme.

4. Another frequent issue that we had to resolve was when students had various sources of funding and fellowships from the university as well as additional external sources. Even though all of our fellows were required to work full time on their doctoral research, they had different levels of income. In addition, university regulations limited the income from internal fellowships to a certain level, leading to a situation where some fellows opted for other fellowships over our programme and eventually dropped out. We found these threats to be a risk to the internal work of our community of practice. If people are at risk of leaving their organic group of entry, this could do harm to the group identity (i.e., "we are not the first option for some of our members"), to the commitment to the group (i.e., "people express a lack of commitment, why should we?"), group activities (i.e., the group was planning an activity where the leaving fellows had an active role), or group prestige (i.e., "people are leaving this programme for some other – maybe better – options"). Group cohesion can also be harmed when the person leaving is a central actor within the group or when he or she had high leadership qualities. In sum, attrition from the group and its activities, especially when other resources allocated have a higher priority, could cause damage to

internal processes of the community of practice. Therefore, strong efforts were made to avoid fellows' attrition from the group. We were pleased that even when fellows received additional fellowships, their dedication to the group's activities remained intact.
5. The Hebrew University is located in four different campuses that are about 30 minutes to an hour apart. Since the fellows were doctoral students in all four campuses, it was difficult to assume they could meet informally on weekdays or evenings. This was one of the reasons we started each meeting with 45 minutes of informal gathering time (with refreshments served). After the session ended, we offered the fellows from other campuses working spaces as well as spaces for informal discussions. Despite this distance constraint, we were surprised to learn that many informal groups were formed by the fellows, based on cohorts or other shared interests.
6. The group's meeting sessions were originally designed to be once every two weeks and only during the semesters (excluding the summer and winter breaks). Each meeting lasted only four hours. This was an extension from the original meeting time that was designed for an hour and a half in the original planning. The additional time allocated for the group meetings was added over the years due to the fellows' requests. It is important to mention that, even now, the slot of four hours is too short and the fellows suggested adding time extensions on various occasions. The decision not to add meeting time resulted from the time constraints expressed by many fellows, especially those working in research laboratories.

These mentioned constraints and complexities were factors that hindered the ability to generate meaningful group activities and, as a result, group cohesion and bonding. We were aware of them and thus looked for other means and practices that could enhance group bonding. In the following section, we discuss a few such means, including expressing appreciation for group members' achievements, holding informal meetings, integrating social projects with academic activities, empowering group members as committed contributors, and generating synergies between the membership activities and the private/family sphere.

Over the years of leading the Hoffman Leadership and Responsibility Programme at the Hebrew University of Jerusalem, we accumulated numerous examples of means applied to enhance group bonding. Among them are:

- Expressing appreciation for group members' achievements – doctoral students, in general, operate on different academic activity dimensions. They conduct research, teach, start publishing their research, apply for fellowships and grants, present their work at conferences, and win various awards of academic recognition. In addition, while they are active in their social volunteering and entrepreneurship activities, they can be recognized by the various stakeholders surrounding them. They can be successful in achieving unique findings in their research; they can be successful in raising funds for their activities; and they can be acknowledged by the media, other organizations, or the university; and so on. At the Hoffman programme, we decided that the fellows' achievements should be formally and openly acknowledged. Therefore, at the beginning of each meeting, we had a short informative opening in which we told the group about the fellows' recent achievements. After the announcements, the fellows provided some background information on their achievements. The group members spontaneously applauded these announcements and added to the culture of a support community. We heard many times from the fellows that these announcements not only generated a spirit of acknowledgement and appreciation but were also sources of information about possible resources and outlets. In addition, they contributed to the accumulation of a strong motivation for continuous hard work and for investment in both their career and the social commitment activities. Since many of the fellows were too modest to talk about their own success, we encouraged the legitimate practice of sharing anonymous positive "gossip" among us. In this way, various bonding and supporting practices were enhanced and legitimized.
- Holding informal meetings – we were surprised to learn that most entering cohort had established a practice of informal gatherings, a few times a year, in one of the fellows' homes. During these gatherings, they would share and eat a potluck dinner and get to know each other. These informal encounters were expressed in close communication between fellows during the formal meetings, and during the breaks, it was apparent that special relations had evolved between cohort members who felt very close to each other.
- Integrating social projects with academic activities – as the programme fellows were also doctoral students conducting frontier

research in many different disciplines, many were able to integrate some of their academic-based knowledge into their social-based projects. This called for some creativity with regards to the translation of their academic knowledge to community-based social activities that could be conducted by them. Beyond their own activities, there was always a possibility that such projects could become a "magnet" that would facilitate the recruitment of additional students and attract them to volunteer in the project under the guidance and supervision of the doctoral student.

- Empowering group members as committed contributors – the various projects described in Chapter 6 of this book originate from the fellows' intrinsic motivation and commitment to what they perceived as important, worthy, and of added value to society. As such, these activities did not usually require external rewards. However, once a community of practice was involved in sharing information on the fellows' various activities, there came a spillover of energies that were highly inspiring. It is important that the activities, even if they were internally motivated, were acknowledged by others. This was especially true when the "others" were perceived as significant actors for the fellows. Comments, expressions of support, suggestions for additional activities, or connections to others who could be of assistance (funding, capabilities, etc.) were very important for any social entrepreneurs establishing a social venture.

  It is therefore of great importance to establish group sessions that allow fellows to describe their projects and become empowered by feedback, acknowledgement, contacts, and information received from other fellows. These feedback sessions were not intended to enhance the intrinsic commitment that existed already but to provide further inspiration and aspiration in the development of their projects.

- Generating synergies between the membership activities and the private/family sphere – as mentioned above, most of the doctoral students in Israel are older than their counterparts in other countries due to the long military service and pre-university work. As a result, many doctoral students are already married and have one or two young children. Many of the fellows in the programme had at least one baby during their 3-year participation in the programme. Therefore, the fellows' families were also an important part of their daily activities. This meant that the programme had to be sensitive to the fact that the family and children sphere of the fellows' lives had to be acknowledged in the programme.

The programme's initial policy was that once a fellow had a baby, the baby was welcome to join the mother or father as long as the parent felt a need to stay with the baby and bring him or her to the group meetings. The group celebrated the new baby by acknowledging its arrival in an electronic announcement. Then, during the father/mother's first session of the group meetings, the programme's members welcomed the new parent, and the baby was given a gift. Many fellows who were young mothers came to the meetings with their babies for a period of about 1–3 months. They left the room only if the baby was crying in a way that was causing interruptions, and they returned once the baby was quiet again. This welcoming approach to parents led to a high commitment to the programme and close family-like relations among the fellows. In addition, the fellows knew that if a young child got sick and the parents had no other option, they could bring the child and let him or her read or paint in one of the rooms while the fellows participated in the sessions.

The walls of the meeting room were made of glass and thus were transparent. Hence, if children were joining their parents, they had the space to relax while seeing, through the glass walls, their parents convening. Establishing these family-friendly policies led to a higher level of commitment to the programme and closer social circles among the fellows. I will always remember how one fellow came to the group meetings with her third baby only two weeks after he was born. The baby passed between the hands of the various fellows as they shared in the mother's happiness, and they were willing to help her with anything she needed during the session and beyond. This was a real heart-warming scene.

- Establishing the formal setting for flexible activities – after four years of operation, the programme was granted a physical location – a centre – for its activities. The centre included quiet working rooms where the fellows were invited to work by themselves or with others, a large meeting room, a small kitchen area with refreshments and places to eat, and some quiet relaxation areas with sofas to rest on or to gather for group discussions.

The flexible space setting was also used to conduct our annual graduation event with the programme donors, the university president and rector, and the fellows and their families. The possibility of rearranging the tables and moving them out of the meeting room allowed us to use them as dining tables, and we were able to arrange the room for a formal graduation event. We used the kitchen area to serve the food, and the other flexible areas were used for a reception, a small refreshment place, and for dancing after the formal graduation event.

During some sessions (such as our unconference sessions), the flexible areas allowed space for alternative activities, such as a self-defence class conducted by two of the fellows, an acting session conducted by one of the fellows, and a folk dancing class taught by one of the fellows. This community-based learning included special events where the sharing of practices, outside the range of academic or social-responsibility activities, added an experience of holistic quality to the group members as well as a deep appreciation for the wide range of capabilities they had obtained and shared.

Overall, with the aim of not only analytically discussing the need for change in academia but also advocating for and spelling out possibilities for such change towards ACL, we present here the example of the Hoffman Leadership and Responsibility Programme at the Hebrew University. In Chapter 6, we describe specific projects initiated and led by the Hoffman Leadership and Responsibility Programme fellows who exemplify ACL.

> Without scientific progress the national health would deteriorate; without scientific progress we could not hope for improvement in our standard of living or for an increased number of jobs for our citizens; and without scientific progress we could not have maintained our liberties against tyranny. (Vannevar Bush, *Science – The Endless Frontier*, Report to the US President Roosevelt, July 1945)

## NOTE

1. In Israel, there is a mandatory army service requirement. As a result, students can only enter university at age 20–23. In addition, the higher education system in Israel is based on three consecutive degrees: Bachelor, Master, and Ph.D. As a result, many doctoral students are much older than their counterparts in the world. On top of this, the norms for early family establishment and early childbirth are strong in Israel. All these factors combined lead to the fact that many doctoral students are married with children.

# 6. ACL projects in an ACL-inspired programme: examples from the Hoffman programme

In this chapter, we provide examples for academic commitment and leadership (ACL) volunteering projects that were designed by ten Hoffman fellows individually. We have chosen to describe only projects that were related to the main academic discipline of the doctoral student in order to show how many areas of academic work can have an impact on the external needs of society. To offer the greatest spectrum possible, in this chapter, we describe ACL projects that included activities in a few different areas such as education, policy, health, and youth activities. The ACL projects were developed either before joining the programme, during the programme, or during the post-programme activities by the programme's fellows. The description of these ACL projects was gathered from the Hoffman programme fellows. All project descriptions were confirmed and approved by the Hoffman fellows involved, and they were invited to modify or approve the text. All but one (who is currently a faculty member at HUJI) were happy to be introduced by their names and the names of their leading collaborators, and all were very proud of their achievements. We thank them for sharing their ideas and insights with us.

Obviously, these ACL project descriptions offer only an abstract and thus only a small part of the details. There is a great deal to learn from their experience about the formation of the project, the development and maintenance of the project's activities, the gathering of funding resources, and the attraction of additional volunteering participants to the project. Only one person managed and operated some of the projects, but most of them attracted many additional participants who contributed to the success of the projects and, at a later stage, needed a salaried CEO. However, all these are beyond the scope of this chapter.

The ACL projects were initiated by the fellows and were based on the academic expertise of our fellows coupled with their social commitment. Some of these projects became attractive to additional fellows and students who enthusiastically joined the project and activities. Each of the ACL projects we describe below includes a description of the main goal, the social group towards which the project was designed, and the main area of focus of the programme's activity.

## Project 1: Providing In-House Pharmacology Expert Advice to Elderly People

Goal: Assist elderly people with health-related issues
Social group: Elderly Holocaust survivors
Area of activity: Expert advice in pharmacology

The first example of an ACL project was planned, designed, and formed by Dr. Gali Umschweif (currently a postdoctoral fellow at the Rockefeller University). While attending the programme, Gali was a doctoral student at the department of pharmacology at the Hebrew University. Gali was an outstanding student who had also taught in large classes at the pharmacology department and the medical school, and she was a very valued teacher. Her grandparents were both in related research areas. Gali's grandmother, Natalia Umschweif, was a pharmacist, and her grandfather, Bernard Umschweif, had a Ph.D. and had conducted research in a group involved in developing the vaccine for typhus.[1] Both grandparents had perished during the Holocaust, and she grew up with her father's stories of their legacy and the pain of their loss. Her father managed to survive the Holocaust and raised his family in Israel.

While she was a fellow at the programme, Gali was interested in expressing her commitment to improve the well-being of Holocaust survivals. By now, over 50 years after the Holocaust, all survivors are elderly people, and many have been sick and are treated by many different drugs prescribed to them by physicians. Gali's project was based on her expertise in pharmacy science and her ties to many BA-level students whom she taught. She started by approaching the National Holocaust Institute and asked for its permission to visit elderly Holocaust survivors who lived in her area. Once she received this permission, she set appointments with these people and asked them to prepare the list of the medications they were receiving for her visit. During her visit with them, she reviewed all of the medications prescribed and checked the degree to which they were in conflict or may have caused unnecessary side effects that the general practitioner/physician was not aware of. She found out that many of the elderly people she visited were taking excessive amounts of medications and that these were not always needed. In fact, a combination of the many different drugs was possibly poisoning them and causing great discomfort. Her goal was to study closely the list of medications and their dosages, and she would then write a long letter to the main physician with the recommendation for modifying the list of prescribed medications so that any unnecessary side effects could be prevented.

The project benefited from the combination of expert knowledge and her commitment to the improved well-being of the group she worked with. Once she had started, the head of her programme heard about it and became very enthusiastic in trying to incorporate such voluntary practice for undergraduate and graduate students in the school. This led to the establishment of a larger programme where students were asked to contribute time, knowledge, and effort towards this goal and felt rewarded by their ability to combine academic interest with social responsibility projects.

The programme has been operating for over eight years in the area of Jerusalem and is very successful. It not only offers a synergetic integration between students, research students, and faculty members but also generates a new line of exchange between many local physicians and university students. Such programmes offer a unique added value where universities and their academic leaders can contribute in an exclusive and unique way to stakeholders who need their contribution.

**Project 2: The Revolution Orchestra**

Goal: Create and perform original and creative musically-focused events combined with other performing arts
Social group: Any audience with a special cultural appreciation and interest in creative and original performance arts (some with a special attention on youth-oriented projects)
Area of activity: Creative and innovative musical events that combine other performing arts through collaborations with various artists such as actors, dancers, animators, video artists, VJs, and DJs

The second example of an ACL project is by Dr. Roy Oppenheim. His project led to the establishment and development of "The Revolution Orchestra", dedicated to the dissemination of music and culture in order to promote innovation and creativity in performance arts among young and adult audiences. Roy – the fellow who founded the orchestra – was a doctoral student of music and philosophy of education. He was also a professional orchestra conductor and a pianist from his earlier studies. With a group of other students of music, he formed a small orchestra 15 years ago. The expressed philosophy he was committed to was developing experimental musical events that are creative and innovative, yet always appealing to mass audiences, with a main focus on young adults and youth.

The orchestra developed numerous projects, of which we will describe only three here. All were produced from concept to final execution by the orchestra. In one performance, Roy collaborated with other musicians and animation experts who were students in a Jerusalemite art school to write orchestral music with animation shorts. They had another project, "Peter and the Wolf: the True Story", where, after performing the classical music to the Oscar-winning movie *Peter and the Wolf*, an actor, accompanied by a new score written for the orchestra, provided an alternative version of the story where the wolf is presented as the true victim of the story and his point of view and motivations are better understood. The end of the story is associated with a peaceful understanding and respect between Peter and the wolf. This project was able to bring children closer to classical music while offering a less traumatizing understanding of the end of the story narrated in the original composition. In the third project, the orchestra composed a musical interpretation for a children's story written by a leading national author that was able to combine the love for reading original Israeli fiction books with the appreciation of music, accompanied by a children's chorus that played characters from the plot and sang the various parts.

### Project 3: Informing Farmers about the Needs of Cows – an Educational Project

Goal: Reduce stress and improve the quality of life for cows in dairy farms
Social group: Workers in large dairy farms
Area of activity: Offer education and share research-based information to reduce stress and improve cow well-being

Dr. Roi Mandel (former Hoffman fellow) and Dr. Sivan Lacker (DVM) designed a project aimed at educating farmers on low-stress handling methods and the behavioural needs of cows in order to improve cow well-being. In this project, Dr. Roi Mandel and Dr. Sivan Lacker, a colleague currently in the private sector, developed a tutorial kit (including Power Point presentations, videos, and "hands-on" practice) based on academic research conducted at the School of Veterinary Medicine, the Hebrew University, and several leading animal welfare research groups, and then tested it on a farm. Later, they ran a teaching pilot in dairy farms and a few kibbutzim, and they held seminars at the farms with all of the farm staff members, including temporary and part-time members. The project has now been successfully implemented in various dairy farms in Israel. The service is still offered by his colleague but is no longer free of charge. Dr. Mandel is using a different approach and is developing new methods to share knowledge on cow behaviour to an even wider audience, notably through free online videos made by animal welfare students in his class, dedicated to farmers and the general public, in Israel and Switzerland.[2] The project is now successfully implemented in various dairy farms in Israel.

**Project 4: Website for Teaching Aids for Science and Technology (STS) Teachers**

Goal: Establish a website facility with teaching tools on mathematical and scientific topics
Social group: Science and maths teachers on all levels
Area of activity: Educational supportive tools

The fourth ACL project example was established by Dr. Orit Elgavi-Hershler, a scientist of brain research, who expressed great commitment to teaching science and maths in a friendly manner to all levels of students (from the kindergarten to high school level). In addition, she wanted to offer teaching tools to teachers that could assist them in making science and maths education fun and interesting for students. She established a small community of academic scientists who shared this interest with her, and together they developed a website platform where teachers could download a wide range of science and maths activities for use in the classroom in Hebrew. The website offers free access to materials in a large range of topics including art, geography, science, astronomy, psychology, creative thinking, logic-based inquiries, and so on. To date, many teachers and students benefit from the wealth of various ideas that keep students interested and generate enthusiasm for learning.

## Project 5: Starcatcher Community Theatre in English[3]

Goal: Provide community cohesion through participation in cultural events, an artistic outlet for non-professionals, training, and mentorship for young talent
Social group: English-speaking adults and young adults in the community
Area of activity: Adaptation of plays in English and producing them with community members for other community members

This fifth ACL project aimed to establish a community theatre where community members rehearsed and then performed annual plays for the community. Yaeli Greenblatt, a Hoffman fellow and a HU doctoral student at the English department, is one of three founders of the theatre and was the artistic director. Her founding collaborators are Jeff Rosenschein and Eli Kaplan-Wildmann.

The project is twofold: it created a small group of performing arts individuals who could practice their craft in a supportive environment, become more accepting of each other's differences (e.g., age, religion, experience, and background), work together on a new play every year, and then carry out several performances so as to share their work within the community. Thus, the project enabled the formation of a cohesive community group that further offered community-based cultural events. These included two circles of community cohesiveness processes: one of a community of performing arts lovers and one of cultural appreciators.

In this ACL project, all participants – onstage, backstage, and production participants – are operating largely on a volunteer basis. The theatre community offered a social base for many individuals who were recent emigrants or were considering emigration, by providing a foundation for social life in Israel.

## Project 6: Opportunities for Reassessing Gender Bias in Choosing High School Specialization

Goal: Reassess gender bias in choosing high school specialization
Social group: 10th grade high school students
Area of activity: Exposure to gender biases and promotion of an individualized reassessment of subject area and educational choices

This ACL project was envisioned, planned, and designed by Dr. Galit Agmon and Dr. Edden Gerber, both past Hoffman fellows. Their gender-bias reassessment project was most successful and attracted great interest from schools and high school students as well as university students who volunteered to participate in this project. The main idea behind this project was that there is a gender bias for high school students, in terms of a focus on the sciences or humanities, when choosing specializations during their last two years in high school. To overcome these biases, the workshop established by Galit and her colleagues focused on introducing gender biases and their effects and impact on the disciplinary decisions made by students.

Two different workshops, for female and male high school students, were planned and introduced just before the students were asked to present their preferences to their teachers. The project drew a great deal of attention, and in less than a year many schools across the country asked to join the project and offered these workshops to their students. The growth of the project was so impressive that they started to raise funding, hired a CEO with a salary, and listed themselves as an NGO.

**Project 7: The Education Law Clinic**

Goal: Offer free legal counselling regarding elementary schools – more generally, using legal tools for promoting educational equality through the representation of individual parents and students, drafting legislation, and promoting policy

Social group: People in need in the community who can benefit from legal counselling in various areas with regards to the elementary educational systems in Israel

Area of activity: Families with children in the educational system

Law clinics are another example of an ACL project, and such clinics operate in every law school in Israeli universities. In general, law clinics offer free legal services and advice to marginalized individuals and use legal tools to promote human rights. A fellow doctoral student, Dr. Tammy Harel Ben-Shahar (currently an assistant professor at Haifa University in Israel), who had both an interest and expertise in the area of education, developed the specific area of interest. Her research was in education law, and based on her expertise, she partnered with a legal clinic and an NGO working on education rights to establish a hotline that offered legal aid to parents of K-12 school students whose rights and entitlements were not respected by the Ministry of Education, or who were discriminated against by schools and education authorities. The service recipients included parents of students with special needs, parents of students from different ethnic or religious groups, and students from low-income families. Knowledge of the legal aspects of the educational system, the rules of the Ministry of Education, and the policies of the various schools in the public system could assist parents who have experienced hardships with the system concerning their children, and this was offered by the Education Law Clinic. Additionally, the team drafted new legislation meant to promote educational equality in Israel and participated in various activities for policy change in the area of education.

**Project 8: A Pro-Peace Social Entrepreneurship – "Kids 4 Peace"**

Goal: Peace-facilitating social and educational youth movement
Social group: Youth from Jewish, Muslim, and Christian religious backgrounds in Jerusalem
Area of activity: Collaborative social, cultural, and educational activities for youth from the three religious groups

With the goal of early socialization for inter-religion joint social activities, the "Kids 4 Peace" project created a youth movement and educational activities that brought together youth and their parents from the three religions. This ACL programme is not based on an academic discipline but a philosophical and ideological understanding of how peace can be enhanced in the daily lives of youth. The programme is comprised of weekly meetings during the school year and a camp in Israel and the US during the summer. Dr. Yakir Englander, one of the founders of the programme in Jerusalem, was a doctoral student of Jewish studies. Yakir felt that kids from various religions can only grow up to become peace-enhancing adults when they are trained to be peace activists. This can be achieved by understanding their religious narratives as well as their beliefs and they are working together for change in their schools and community. This project and the vision behind it are still in operation today (over 15 years now), and many children from the three religions and their families have been participating over the years.

**Project 9: Jewish–Arabic Collaborative Reading Sessions of Religious Writing**

Goal: Bring together Jewish and Arabic scholars of religious studies
Social group: Jewish and Arabic scholars

Area of activity: Collaborative learning and understanding of the other group

With the aim of exposing alternative religious writings from the three religious denominations (i.e., Islam, Judaism, and Christianity), the group of scholars was formed by one of our Hoffman fellows. This ACL project was designed by a scholar of Jewish thought (a professor currently teaching at the Hebrew University). The project was arranged for weekly meetings where scholars from the three religions gathered in order to read and discuss religious writing from the various religions. Additional scholars were invited to join the group. Such close learning group sessions established closer relations between the members and created higher levels of sensitivity and openness to the various religions.

**Project 10: Community Gardens for Elderly Citizens who Emigrated from Ethiopia to Israel**

Goal: Provide adaptive social practices for Ethiopian emigrants that bring them closer to their ancestors' agricultural skills
Social group: Recent emigrants from Ethiopia to Israel
Area of activity: Teach and learn agriculture capabilities of ancestors and community-sharing resources

There is a large Ethiopian community in the city around the Faculty of Agriculture's campus of the Hebrew University. Among these, there are many elderly emigrants. The Faculty of Agriculture's campus has a field for community gardening that offers the surrounding public an opportunity to garden. Prof. Alon Samach, a professor of agriculture and fellow from the Faculty of Agriculture, and Naama Teboul, a current fellow in the programme, established this ACL project in order to facilitate community empowerment through collaborative gardening and sharing of the agricultural goods for the Ethiopian elderly. During their participation, they benefit from physically rewarding activities (walking from home for about 30 minutes), coupled with social encounters with other farmers, their family members who joined (including grandchildren), and the students. The project also connects them to the cultural origins of agriculture work in Ethiopia and allows for intergenerational transformation of knowledge and expertise. In addition, a double learning loop became apparent: the volunteering students learned about Ethiopian agriculture, and the Ethiopians learned about new agriculture methods.

## SUMMARY OF SORTS ...

We have provided here ten short examples of ACL projects that were established or developed by Hoffman fellows before or during their participation in the programme. Most of the ACL projects were related to the main academic discipline of the fellows in various ways. We have selected these projects since they are still ongoing. The lengthy survival of these projects (some are 14 years old) provides evidence of how valuable and meaningful they are in identifying an important need, attracting additional volunteers, growing and adjusting to the changing needs, and gathering the needed funding for continuation. The Hoffman programme offered only initial organizational consulting support, and all further resources were gathered by the fellows and their collaborators.

Obviously, there are many additional projects in the Hoffman programme that can add value to society through the use of ACL, especially in the field of education. Maths students were present who gave special support and new teaching methods to maths teachers. Others brought kids from underprivileged families to campus and organized special teaching and exposure sessions for them in order to enhance their curiosity and sense of ability, while some assisted high school students in various learning areas. Also, some fellows assisted the Arab students with their Hebrew writing stills because the teaching was in Hebrew, while others assisted new emigrants with their adjustment needs.

> Universities have a dual responsibility for leading changes and responding to emerging needs and expectations of society. (Global University Leaders Council, The Hamburg Declaration "Rebuilding the University–Society Relationships", June 2019)

## NOTES

1. Typhus is carried by body lice and fleas, and it was an epidemic in both world wars due to low hygienic conditions. Gali's grandfather, who held a Ph.D. in chemistry, worked in Prof. Rudolf Weigl's lab, and under the Nazi occupation they were forced to continue the research first in their hometown of Lewow and then in Auschwitz. Since the Nazis were highly interested in a vaccine for their soldiers in the east, they kept her father, who was only 5, alive in the camp for two years until liberation. Gali's grandfather died in the camp, and her grandmother lived to walk the death march together with Gali's father and saw the liberation. Ironically, she died from typhus a few days after. A book has been written on this research group

called *The Fantastic Laboratory of Dr. Weigl: How Two Brave Scientists Battled Typhus and Sabotaged the Nazis.*
2. See YouTube channel: https://www.youtube.com/user/ParadigmaProject.
3. The following is their described mission statement: "Starcatcher is a non-profit volunteer-based organization. We believe in high-quality theater, as well as in the capacity for art to create a sense of community in Jerusalem, whether by creating social links between emigrants; among new and veteran Israelis, or by creating a sense of purpose and belonging for members and audiences alike. Our vision is to continue advancing high-quality theater in Jerusalem, while mentoring emerging young artists."

# 7. Concluding comments and reflections: new opportunities for university–society relations

This book engages with a contemporary challenge: how is the university to further involve itself with, and anchor itself within, local and global society? How is the university, as academia's prime and oldest organizational form, to meet the many expectations levied upon it nowadays? These multiple expectations include the following: to contribute; to instruct, educate, and enlighten; to excel; to creatively break through conventions and produce knowledge including *useful* knowledge; to be inclusive and open; to adhere to strict standards of ethics and justice; and to be sustainable and well managed. For academicians, the challenge is significant because we regard academic autonomy and independence to be the principle that nourishes all academic accomplishments. In *Homo Academicus* Pierre Bourdieu writes about this dual position of academicians. He writes (1988, p. 1):

> In choosing to study the social world in which we are *involved*, we are obliged to confront, in *dramatized* form as it were, a certain number of epistemological problems, all related to the question of the difference between practical knowledge and scholarly knowledge, and particularly to the special difficulties involved first in breaking with inside experience and then in reconstructing the knowledge which has been obtained by means of this break.

In this passage, as in this reflexive epitome as a whole, Bourdieu conveys this inside–outside role of academicians: we critique social conventions, hear about social role and impact, while also advocating further social engagement of universities.

In this book, our purpose is to replace the binary language of boundaries by counterposing the ivory tower and autonomy against utility and engagement. To replace this binary perspective, we propose a new model for the public role of a university, namely academic commitment and leadership (ACL). Through our essays herein on the history of university–society relations and on the hold that corporate social responsibility (CSR) has on the engagement of organizations with society, we develop the model of ACL, which we define as an explicit and strategic orientation of the university towards the public good and social agenda issues. Specifically, and as noted in several passages throughout the book, ACL calls for a reorientation of the academic commitment towards advancing the public good and social agenda and towards fostering leadership of social change as a distinct and integral goal of academic education. ACL is coming at the heels of, and thus shadowing, the for-profit practice of CSR, yet ACL is distinctly linked with the university and its longstanding ethos of science, creativity, and the social impact of various sorts. As described in Chapter 3, ACL is distinct from and supplementary to universities' focus on commercialization, or otherwise on economic or technological development and production, which is a focus captured in the articulation of the university's third mission. Rather, ACL is driven by academicians and scientists, hence, it is a "bottom-up" model for responsibility for the public good; and, last, ACL is (to be) institutionalized as an integral element in university operations, practices, mechanisms, and routines, from promotion criteria, to curricular emphasis, to funding. In these ways, ACL is the emergent fourth academic mission.

This book defines, describes, analyses, and exemplifies ACL. Following an introduction to the concept and the conceptual language of our work (Chapter 1), we proceed to describe the historiography of the university's public role, thus placing ACL and contemporary challenges to university–society relations within the context of the millennium-long process of change to the university (Chapter 2). With that, we argue that contemporary debates surrounding university–society relations are imprinted by this long history, simultaneously enabling changes to the university by revealing its resilience through the ages while also constraining its change because of the stickiness of academic heritage. Seeing the evolution of the university throughout the millennium as a process of adaptive transformation, in light of changing societal conditions, we argue that the university's adoption of ACL reflects not only the longstanding commitment of science and academia to the public good but is also directly influenced by the success of CSR as the contemporary model of contribution to and engagement with society (Chapter 3). Chapter 4 offers an analytic-cum-illustrative way to define ACL: we provide examples of the many current practices that convey ACL, at universities worldwide – from law clinics to "town and gown" programmes – and proceed to pose Albert Einstein as a hero figure for ACL. With that, we argue that while ACL is emerging as an explicitly strategic identity of a university, academicians and universities have taken actions that follow ACL's "tune." Therefore, ACL is not to replace or overshadow the previous three missions of universities – teaching, research, and production – but rather, ACL themes are infused into all university actions. To further demonstrate the potency of ACL as an organizational principle, we describe the Hoffman Leadership and Responsibility Programme, for doctoral students at the Hebrew University of Jerusalem, which is our professional home (Chapters 5 and 6). By describing the Hoffman programme and several of its student-led ACL-inspired projects, we intend to inspire future ACL initiatives. This chapter is intended to comment on the future of ACL and on university–society relations inspired by ACL.

## MOVING FORWARD

CSR is casting a long shadow over organized acts of social responsibility. The premise of our work on ACL is indeed that the contemporary (re-)orientation of universities towards engagement with communities, concern with societal challenges, and impact on the public good is framed by the legacy of CSR. This, we argued, is furthered by the rise of managerialism in universities: when more universities borrow management models and organizational practices, structures, and behaviours from the sphere of corporate for-profit organizations, the universities cast more of their longstanding societal involvement into the mould of CSR. ACL is an attempt to break with this pattern, namely with the institutional inertia that drives universities to confine their societal engagement and impact to the scope of CSR. While ACL reflects upon CSR, ACL, we argue, builds on an inherent feature of universities – that is, their evolving legacy of relations with society.

Still, seeing that CSR has a decades-long track record, can universities learn from the charges levied against CSR? Specifically, are critiques raised against CSR relevant for challenging ACL? While ACL is inspired by CSR and spurred by the transformation of universities into organizations (see Krücken and Meier, 2006), we previously established that CSR and ACL are very different and that the relations between them are not a simple outcome of translation. Seeing this premise, here we debate whether the critiques levied against CSR are relevant for ACL and, if so, how they might be answered.

CSR has encountered various criticisms from different angles. For example, Freeman and Velamuri (2006) have been critical in presenting various issues, ranging from budgeting and accounting of CSR activities within the corporation to issues of organizational honesty, strategic understanding, and attention – that is, how many corporations, irrespective of their intent, are honest about their possible lack of progress in terms of corporate responsibility? Additionally, with regards to public relations and media coverage issues, how many enterprises admit that they adopt CSR only because of press, media, and watchdog pressure? In the context of ACL, we agree that the issue of a university's integrity and strategic understanding of ACL activities should be questioned and taken into consideration. This is especially true for ACL activities that are conducted from the top down. Here, we mean that the decisions on which activities to pursue and support institutionally, as well as whether they are strategically aligned with the advantages and capabilities of the university, come from the top administration of the university.

Out of the many critiques offered on CSR we picked a few, and in the next section we discuss the relevance of these critiques on CSR to ACL. Obviously, not every critique on CSR can be simply "translated" to ACL, but it is important for us to hold these against the "mirror" of ACL in order to open the discussion on potential or actual problems with the decisions and operation and the management of ACL.

1. The first critique we revisit here is that there is no agreement on the definition of CSR: what acts it stands for in terms of social responsibility and what organizations are designated this responsibility. With that, this critique also challenges the authenticity of CSR as a socially minded act.

Whereas CSR is also practiced as a strategic corporate plan, and has been for decades, ACL is an emergent trend in universities. Therefore, regarding the context of ACL, we agree that, aside from the definition we offer in this book, there is currently no clear definition of ACL and the range of possible actions is wide and diverse. In our view, ACL is becoming an emerging mission and, as such, is still being defined. However, we claim that it is already more focused and defined than CSR has become after several decades of action. One reason could be the result of the institutionalization of organizations' activities for the good of society in general and thus a more focused interest of the university in ACL. The other reason could be the fact that universities were always taking actions for the benefit of society through their initial three missions: teaching, conducting research that can advance the knowledge and the needs of society, and advancing commercialization of this knowledge for the benefit of society.

Thus, ACL actions taken by universities are not challenging the authenticity of their social actions but offering new pathways for various actions for the benefit of society. The actions can be taken by enlarging the scope of teaching (e.g., maths professors who are volunteering their time for teaching high school students in certain areas where the level of education is relatively low and thus are inspiring the students to aim for enrolment in higher education). In the area of research, many university professors offer internship and training options for high school students in their laboratories with the goal of attracting them to academic research and socializing them into their research teams. The third mission of commercialization can also take the motivation of benefiting society. This can be done by charging low royalties from industrial firms or offering non-exclusive licensing (so as to allow more firms to access the technology) in the widespread use of a novel technology developed by the university for advancing drug development, (e.g., Oliver and Liebeskind (2009) showed how Stanford University had the patent license for recombinant DNA technology, which was developed by Cohen and Boyer at Stanford University in 1973 but was then licensed very broadly and at low cost to commercial users). The fourth mission of ACL is, in fact, a form of variation on the first three missions with the option for novel and creative contributions. The fact that universities have always conducted some form of commitment and leadership depicts the authenticity of the social actions taken by universities under the mission of ACL.

With regards to the level within the organization that is in charge of ACL, our model claims that ACL actions can be conducted from the top down – defined and coordinated by the university management – and bottom up – as emerging from choices made by advanced students or professors who wish to add a volunteering activity related to their academic teaching, research, or commercialization activities. Thus, universities are advantaged when working time can be flexible and agency actions can be facilitated at any level. There is no need to have a designated office for ACL; rather, one should assume a loosely integrated network of volunteering actions in different venues.

2. The second critique we revisit is that corporations have no capacity or experience in the field of social responsibility and thus should concentrate on their prime expertise and relative advantage.

Recognizing universities as sites for teaching, research, and commercialization of knowledge, this critique against CSR can also be levied against ACL. In fact, at the early stages of the third mission, many academicians argued against this mission, in that it drives them far beyond their academic skills and capacities (Nelson (2001) offered an interesting review of the early history of university commercialization). Similarly, many academicians have griped about ACL and claimed that ACL should not be regarded as missing from universities for many reasons. Claims include the fact that universities should concentrate on what they do best; that universities do not have the funding and the administration for social responsibility activities; or that universities should leave the care of these activities to the public or the non-profit sectors. We respond to these protests in the following section.

3. The third critique we revisit here is that firms should avoid general CSR activities and their activities should best be done in direct relation to corporations' prime task and the expertise. For example, banks should concentrate on financial CSR and offer tutorials and consultations to families on budget monitoring and saving plans.

With regards to ACL, this critique would be translated to the claim that academicians should also link between ACL and the university's core capacities – within the framework of the teaching and research missions and perhaps with the commercialization mission. However, because academic institutions are particularly diffused and diverse (by teaching and research discipline; by research vs. technical vs. teaching schools; and by wholly integrated universities vs. specialized universities), so should their various translations/applications of ACL. Nevertheless, as apparent from the examples provided in this book (Chapter 6), most ACL activities are mainly related to the two initial missions of the university (e.g., teaching and research).

4. The fourth critique we revisit is that CSR initiatives should be built into the organization's budget so that it is possible to trace its auctioning through the structure, and it centres on the normative question of the organization's profitability and if there should be a line of profit for CSR operations.

Clearly, some ACL activities may need to be budgeted. This could mean that universities need to assign a budget for ACL-related expenses. However, these do not need to be direct expenses. Fellowships designed specifically for students involved in ACL activities can be one indirect way to fund ACL activities. Other activities may include courses that involve community activities as part of the tasks expected of students.

For example, Amalya Oliver (the first author) taught a course for three years that was funded by the Israeli Council of Higher Education and dedicated to combining theory and research with volunteering time in a community not-for-profit organization in the area of gender or ethnicity empowerment. The students participated in formal lessons on related topics, completed reading assignments, and were asked to write a paper in which they applied the theories and research they learned to their volunteer experiences in the organization. The data used by the students were supplemented with the following: interviews with organizational employees and volunteers, as well as with members, service recipients, or clients; internal documents of the organization; and observations in various activities and events. Thus, no university-level budgetary costs were associated with the ACL activities of the students in this course. In addition, all students received a modest scholarship that covered their main expenses, which was sponsored by the Israeli Council of Higher Education. Therefore, this example illustrates how other stakeholders, such as the government, may have an interest in supporting universities for their ACL activities. This is done with the understanding that there is a double loop of ACL here – first, there is a direct contribution to society by voluntary activities in the not-for-profit sector by students. The second, long-term effect is the impact of this activity on the long-term socialization of students and their understanding of the importance of ACL and the not-for-profit sector. While acting within the ACL frame, students internalize and adapt the norms and values that combine giving and learning. Overall, this teaching act embodies the principles of ACL: it harnesses academic knowledge, training, and mentorship to impact the public good.

Regarding the following critical point – profits from ACL – this mission is not one undertaken with an aim for profit. If any profits accrue, they should be put back into the ACL funding in order to pursue additional ACL activities.

Debates around these issues are venues for further innovation and change of ACL. It is clear that ACL, as much as we offer a variety of exemplar cases from contemporary academia – at the levels of individual scientists, universities, and national academic systems – is still evolving and taking new directions as the process unfolds. There are many changes and opportunities for its expansion, and it is important that it remains an open pursuit of goals and preferences at this stage.

## TAKING ACTION: COMMITMENT AND LEADERSHIP AS STRATEGY

In this spirit of ACL echoing yet transforming the discourse of CSR, we redefine the missions of universities. Not only are we calling for explicating ACL as the fourth mission of universities in the current day, but we also explicitly revisit its institutional inspiration, namely CSR. Consequently, by revisiting Carroll's (1991) definition of CSR and his illustration of the pyramid model of CSR (2016, p. 410; see Chapter 3), we outline the tiers of ACL. In Table 7.1, we propose a scheme to describe the three premises that are at the heart of ACL. These can be seen in the left-hand column.

First, ACL is premised on universities being economically sustainable, thus expressing their commitment to the public good and their leadership in public affairs by also being prudent in their use of public and other funds. Second, ACL is also premised on universities being upstanding institutional citizens, thus expressing their commitment and leadership not only through the obvious adherence to the law but also by actively promoting an agenda. Among these societal agendas are the promotion of political and civil rights and protections and, specifically, the reframing of access to higher education as a civic right. Third, ACL is premised on universities being generous towards the public, thus expressing their commitment and leadership by being attentive to changing societal conditions, by bringing academic goods to public use, and by engaging with the public to set a civic, as well as academic, agenda. Such premises are actionable items for universities: the right-hand column in Table 7.1 lists several examples for activities that universities are, and should be, taking to act upon their commitment to the public good and their leadership in public affairs.

Importantly, we stress that actionable commitment and actionable leadership are not evenly set across these analytic tiers of the ACL model. Rather, as is marked in the middle column of Table 7.1, although commitment and leadership are "two sides of the same coin" of the fourth mission of the university, the ambitions and plans of universities to bring about public good and to engage with societal challenges are restrained by its limited sovereignty over public affairs. Our visualization here is obviously only an illustration of such differential expressions of com-

Table 7.1  Tiers of ACL

| Premise | Academic Leadership / Academic Commitment | Directions for action: |
|---|---|---|
| Be generous towards the public | | – Proclaiming social justice agenda in the public sphere<br>– Volunteering academic resources (teaching)<br>– Founding and supporting non-profit social ventures for the public good<br>– Contributing to policy planning<br>– Enlisting university resources (personnel, labs) for social emergencies |
| Be upstanding institutional citizen | | – Integrating underrepresented social groups<br>– Promoting fair employment practices<br>– Adhering to ethical codes for research and teaching<br>– Defending citizens' rights and protection against harassment and discrimination<br>– Serving public needs by responding to lacunae in public and governmental services |
| Be economically sustainable | | – Commercializing university-generated knowledge<br>– Partnering and collaborating with public agencies and firms<br>– Prioritizing competitive grant funding for research and teaching<br>– Providing global academic exchange in teaching and research<br>– Offering for-fee services, even if adjusting costs to fit its public mission |

mitment and leadership. It is by design imprecise and aimed at stirring a debate around the extent of universities' engagement with public affairs and the form for such engagement.

## ACL AS A REFLECTION ON THE CHARACTER OF UNIVERSITIES

ACL offers a programmatic tool for universities to follow – one that befits the complexity of societal challenges in the contemporary era. The trend of and call for universities to become more socially engaged, as much as they aim to look outside of academia and focus on societal processes and necessities, is also a point of self-reflection. In this section, we reflect on how universities are evolving and how they *should* evolve. Such reflection calls attention to the pressing issues for contemporary academia: autonomy and freedom, professionalism and scientific norms, and marketization and managerialism. These issues are therefore pertinent to universities adopting the fourth mission of ACL.

ACL confirms that universities are redefining the societal and formal groups with whom they engage, also formally. Into the sphere of direct relations with students, faculty, and partners in industry and government, ACL-driven universities are also engaging with communities in their surrounding town, worldwide populations in need, and organized public. The diversity of partners and constituencies of the 21st-century university stirs discussions about the "who" – namely, who makes the decisions about university adoption and adaptation of ACL and who is the "impactee" of ACL initiatives?

The feature of diffused authority in universities, which is sanctified in the norm of academic freedom and autonomy, must not obscure the power mechanisms by which decisions are being made in universities. This raises the following question: who decides on ACL priorities and sets ACL-motivated plans for universities? In light of the diffused authority structure in universities and the encroachment of professional management and administration on the governance authority of the professoriate, it is up to universities to set their uniquely appropriate format for decision-making about the priorities for ACL. For some universities, decision-making about the priorities for ACL is placed in the hands of the academicians, whereas in other universities, ACL priorities are best set jointly by academicians, students, and university management. In addition, drawing on successful experiences of other civic action initiatives, some universities do, and others should, engage the communities they seek to impact in the process of setting ACL goals and plans. Last, for some national polities where the state and its agencies play a central role in the sector of higher education and academia, universities are advised to also enlist the support and cooperation of political bodies, garner support for the ACL agenda, and safeguard implementation under conditions of state supervision. By articulating who is to chart ACL initiatives for universities and by building a context-specific coalition of partners, universities formalize and thus legitimize ACL as a core mission; most importantly, they better motivate and enlist these various constituencies towards whatever ACL goal and plan they collaboratively set for their university.

In defining the social groups that the university intends to enlist in order to activate its ACL mission, the university is likewise challenged to answer the question, who is an "impactee"? In other words, who are the people, communities and social groups, and organizations and agencies that are to be the recipients of, and partners with, the many action items that the ACL model proposes? A university's commitment and leadership will surely be tested upon such identification of the partners' social characteristics and on its decision on how to engage with each person or social group. The aspiration to do good in the world is tested in these actions. It includes thoughtfulness about the definitions of the "ideal" or "worthy" recipient and partner, decisions on what knowledge is "appropriate" and "useful" to each target group or partner, and identification of strategies and techniques for appropriate engagement and effective impact. Universities today have laid before them the many considerations that shape an appropriate *and* just society-minded vision and strategy.

Seeing these multiple considerations – in regard to the social groups and actors involved in ACL projects – one cannot expect any uniformity of ACL actions by universities. Not only is the university challenged by the diversity of each project's stakeholders or partners, but such partners may have expectations that differ from those that the university and the academicians are interested in or able to provide and answer. Among the different expectations of stakeholders, we also anticipate the possibility of conflicting expectations. Academia adopting ACL should also anticipate some conflicting interests and power struggles among the different stakeholders. Such struggles will have to be resolved by the procedures set by the university, also setting the tone for how social agenda issues are to be negotiated. On this matter of how to resolve struggles, universities may apply the ACL logic. For example, to solve disputes or debates, the university may stand as a model for its collegial and representative decision-making. Although university governance is increasingly formalized and managerialized, the university still maintains its professional – that is, collegial and representative – ethos as its compass. ACL maintains the historic change to the definition of academic autonomy and freedom (see Tapper and Salter, 1995), expanding the normative bounds of the professional community of scholars inside the university and in extension activities. In this way, ACL serves as a strategy for negotiating the expansion and variety of stakeholders for the university's social engagement and impact.

Further pressure on the university's fourth mission comes from the heterogeneity of the academic field across countries and within national spheres. Seeing that ACL is all about social engagement, it is pertinent that it is contextualized (i.e., defined, assessed, and implemented) in relation to its social and institutional contexts. As also discussed in Chapter 3, such contextualizing is in response to the features and composition of stakeholders. Additional contextualizing is in response to the institutional environment. This point echoes Burton Clark's (1978, 2004) description of where university systems of various countries are situated within what he calls the "triangle of coordination" – namely, oriented more towards the state, market, or academic oligarch: Italian academia is oriented primarily towards the triangular angle of the academic oligarchy, Soviet academia is oriented primarily towards the triangular angle of the state, and US academia is oriented primarily towards the triangular angle of the market, with Swedish, French, British, Japanese, and other systems situated within this triangular model. Echoing Clark's model, we too claim that ACL-age academia should indeed be attuned to the context of the policy and society.

If ACL is going to be further adopted and formally implemented as a vision and a strategy for social engagement, must it also be indexed and modelled after other academic missions? In other words, seeing that the academic missions of teaching, research, and tech transfer have been implemented in the matrices of valuation – from scientometric measures to impact factors to teaching evaluations – might this fourth mission of social impact also be indexed? The blooming conversation about the asocial impact of universities has now bred the first set of "impact rankings" by *The Times Higher Education World University Ranking*.[1] These rankings provide evidence that universities' responsibility issues matter greatly to various stakeholders in the institutional environment. These rankings not only depict what is considered valuable but also have an impact on what universities will further advance in order to be ranked highly on these various ranking systems. For example, the SDG 12 ranks universities around the world on responsible consumption and measures universities' approach to the sustainable use of resources.

Other rankings refer to additional ACL activities, including a reference to good health and well-being, and measure universities' research on key diseases and conditions. Others refer to their support for healthcare professions and the health of students and staff (SDG 3) or quality education (SDG 4) and gender equality (SDG 5). With reference to growth and innovation, there are references to decent work and economic growth (SDG 8) as well as industry innovation and infrastructure that measure patenting and spin-off companies founded by universities (SDG 9). Much like other scaling and ranking measures of academic performance and prestige (see Gioia and Corley, 2002; King, 2009; Wedlin, 2006), the quantification, bureaucratization, and rationalization of ACL bring risk to the university's character. The quantification and standardization of measures for ACL are likely to produce a rigid framework for ACL and thus become counter-effective. Therefore, while it is important to highlight the ACL-driven contributions of universities and to celebrate their context-specific varieties, formal scaling of ACL can jeopardize the authentic and bottom-up spirit of ACL.

Among the changes that ACL will bring to universities is also a change to academic labour. One of its direct and immediate effects will be on the definition of academic work and thus on the nature of an academic career. For example, social engagement and impact will become a criterion for academic performance and thus for promotion. Universities will add "public lectures" and "leadership role in public organization" in the same way as they added "registration of patents" to reports of academic work. Likewise, quantifiable markers of social engagement and impact may be added to reporting – by individual academics and by universities alike. While this alignment of the incentive structure of the academic career with ACL will indeed require academicians to become more attuned to social engagement and impact, it will also add to the already long list of expectations from academics. Krücken et al. (2009) described such impact of "extension activities" to the third academic mission on the academic career, identifying "a growing tension between the more general call for additional missions, on the one hand, and the actual activities of academics on the other hand" (p. 144). A similar impact of the "extension activities" of the university's fourth mission will require that the governance of the university and of the profession meets ACL expectations.

In general, these many ACL-driven changes are charting future paths for universities and for the academic study of universities. Universities are deeply rooted in a culture of social engagement; universities also routinely act on such a sense of social engagement. Still, our discussions of ACL chart paths for the future study of university–society relations and of the missions of universities; also, our discussions point to future actions of universities and practices for universities to institutionalize. In our view, the circle of ACL commitment has been largely expanded: it is not particularly a feature of the recent era because both trends – of globalization and social commitment – have risen in parallel and continuously since the middle of the 20th century. However, we anticipate that ACL activities will become even more dominant due to the interest of the younger generation in combining learning and social activism. It takes the forms of an "identity project" (Harré, 2007) as a means to enlarge the social capital (Jarrett et al., 2005) or as a democratic venue towards community change (Ginwright et al., 2006). One of the unique features of universities is that they allow for many academician–student interactions over various societal issues and offer an opportunity for joint ACL practices.

## POSTSCRIPT: WRITING ABOUT UNIVERSITIES' PUBLIC ENGAGEMENT DURING THE CORONAVIRUS GLOBAL PANDEMIC

In the midst of debates about how universities and academicians can help resolve humanity's grand challenges – global warming, immigration cascades, and perils of illiberalism – came the global coronavirus pandemic of 2020. The pandemic made clear that a new era is emerging, requiring a new mode of thinking and acting. This global "perfect storm" of social upheavals comes at a time when universities are enjoying unprecedented success: as David J. Frank and John W. Meyer (2020) note, not only has the institution of the university endured many social changes over a millennium, but today the university is experiencing an unprecedented global expansion, with more universities in more countries educating additional students in other fields. Like no time before, universities also produce more scientific papers, commercialize more knowledge from their labs, and discover new phenomena at a faster rate than ever before. Then, why do universities continue to come under attack as aloof institutions? More to the point of our book here, what can universities do to use their unprecedented performance to impact humanity's plights, specifically at a time of global crisis?

Reflecting on the worldwide response of universities to the coronavirus pandemic, we see additional signs of the success or resilience of the institution of the university. Moreover, we see signs of universities worldwide acting upon what we here define as ACL, or the university mission that befits the grand challenges of world society in the 21st century. In many countries, universities were among the first to assume responsibility in assisting with the facilities needed to cope with the health hazard and to seek remedy. University professors and their students volunteered in aiding with coronavirus testing in their laboratories, helped the hospital staff with medical students, and increased their research efforts to find potential vaccinations, various means of detection, alternative treatments, and so on, which could benefit them during their ongoing research and knowledge. At some universities, academicians were proactive in making themselves available for consulting public agencies on whatever their discipline offered so as to navigate a response to the emergency.

We conclude this book with the main theme we offer, as both analysis of recent trends and as a horizon for universities to walk towards: universities exhibit institutional resilience, while expecting a rejuvenation through their commitment and leadership towards the public good.

## NOTE

1. https://www.timeshighereducation.com/rankings/impact/2019/responsible-consumption-and-production as of February, 2020.

# Bibliography

Aguilera, R. V., Rupp, D. E., Williams, C. A., and Ganapathi, J. (2007). Putting the S back in corporate social responsibility: A multilevel theory of social change in organizations. *Academy of Management Review*, *32*(3), 836–863.

Aguinis, H., and Glavas, A. (2012). What we know and don't know about corporate social responsibility: A review and research agenda. *Journal of Management*, *38*(4), 932–968.

Ahmad, J. (2012). Can a university act as a corporate social responsibility (CSR) driver? An analysis. *Social Responsibility Journal*, *8*(1), 77–86.

Altbach, P. G. (2016). *Global Perspectives on Higher Education*. JHU Press.

Alzyoud, S. A., and Bani-Hani, K. (2015). Social responsibility in higher education institutions: Application case from the Middle East. *European Scientific Journal*, *11*(8), 122–129.

Amaral, A., Jones, G. A., and Karseth, B. (Eds.). (2013). *Governing Higher Education: National Perspectives on Institutional Governance*. Springer Science & Business Media.

Asemah, E. S., Okpanachi, R. A., and Olumuji, E. P. (2013). Universities and corporate social responsibility performance: An implosion of the reality. *African Research Review*, *7*(4), 195–224.

Austin, I., and Jones, G. A. (2015). *Governance of Higher Education: Global Perspectives, Theories, and Practices*. Routledge.

Bacevic, J. (2017). Beyond the third mission: Toward an actor-based account of universities' relationship with society. In H. Ergül and S. Coşar (Eds.). *Universities in the Neoliberal Era: Academic Cultures and Critical Perspectives* (pp. 21–39). Palgrave Macmillan.

Barrow, C. W. (2018). *The Entrepreneurial Intellectual in the Corporate University*. Springer International Publishing.

Berman, E. P. (2011). *Creating the Market University: How Academic Science became an Economic Engine*. Princeton University Press.

Bleiklie, I., Enders, J., Lepori, B., and Musselin, C. (2011). New public management, network governance and university as a changing professional organization. In T. Christensen and P. Lægreid (Eds.). *The Ashgate Companion to New Public Management* (pp. 161–176). Ashgate.

Bok, D. C. (1982). The corporation on campus: Balancing responsibility and innovation. *Change: The Magazine of Higher Learning*, *14*(6), 16–25.

Bok, D. C. (2009). *Beyond the Ivory Tower: Social Responsibilities of the Modern University*. Harvard University Press.

Bolman, L. G., and Gallos, J. V. (2010). *Reframing Academic Leadership*. John Wiley and Sons.

Bomann-Larsen, L., and Wiggen, O. (Eds.). (2004). *Responsibility in World Business: Managing Harmful Side-effects of Corporate Activity*. United Nations University.

Bourdieu, P. (1988). *Homo Academicus*. Stanford University Press.

Bourdieu, P., and Wacquant, L. (2013). Symbolic capital and social classes. *Journal of Classical Sociology*, *13*(2), 292–302.

Bozeman, B. (1987). *All Organizations are Public: Bridging Public and Private Organizational Theories*. Jossey-Bass.

Bozeman, B. (2013). What organization theorists and public policy researchers can learn from one another: Publicness theory as a case-in-point. *Organization Studies*, *34*(2), 169–188.

Brei, V., and Böhm, S. (2011). Corporate social responsibility as cultural meaning management: A critique of the marketing of "ethical" bottled water. *Business Ethics: A European Review*, *20*(3), 233–252.

Burt, R. S. (2004). Structural holes and good ideas. *American Journal of Sociology*, *110*(2), 349–399.

Burt, R. S. (2005). *Brokerage and Closure: An Introduction to Social Capital*. Oxford University Press.

Burt, R. S. (2007). Secondhand brokerage: Evidence on the importance of local structure for managers, bankers, and analysts. *Academy of Management Journal*, *50*(1), 119–148.

Bush, V. (1945). *Science, the Endless Frontier: A Report to the President*. US Government Printing Office.

Campbell, J. L. (2007). Why would corporations behave in socially responsible ways? An institutional theory of corporate social responsibility. *Academy of Management Review*, *32*(3), 946–967.

Campbell, A., and Yeung, S. (1991). Creating a sense of mission. *Long Range Planning*, *24*(4), 10–20.

Carroll, A. B. (1991). The pyramid of corporate social responsibility: Toward the moral management of organizational stakeholders. *Business Horizons*, *34*(4), 39–48.

Carroll, A. B. (1999). Corporate social responsibility: Evolution of a definitional construction. *Business & Society*, *38*(3), 268–295.

Carroll, A. B. (2016). Carroll's pyramid of CSR: Taking another look. *International Journal of Corporate Social Responsibility*, *1*(1), 3.

Cegarra-Navarro, J. G., Reverte, C., Gómez-Melero, E., and Wensley, A. K. (2016). Linking social and economic responsibilities with financial performance: The role of innovation. *European Management Journal*, *34*(5), 530–539.

Cheslock, J. J., and Gianneschi, M. (2008). Replacing state appropriations with alternative revenue sources: The case of voluntary support. *The Journal of Higher Education*, *79*(2), 208–229.

Christensen, T. (2011). University governance reforms: Potential problems of more autonomy? *Higher Education*, *62*(4), 503–517.

Christensen, T., Gornitzka, Å., and Ramirez, F. O. (2019). Reputation management, social embeddedness, and rationalization of universities. In T.

Christensen, Å. Gornitzka, and F. O. Ramirez (Eds.). *Universities as Agencies: Reputation and Professionalization* (pp. 3–39). Springer.

Clark, B. R. (1978). Academic differentiation in national systems of higher education. *Comparative Education Review*, *22*(2), 242–258.

Clark, B. R. (1998). *Creating Entrepreneurial Universities: Organizational Pathways of Transformation*. Elsevier Science.

Clark, B. R. (2004). Delineating the character of the entrepreneurial university. *Higher Education Policy*, *17*(4), 355–370.

Claydon, J. (2011). A new direction for CSR: The shortcomings of previous CSR models and the rationale for a new model. *Social Responsibility Journal*, *7*(3), 405–420.

Colish, M. L. (1997). *Medieval Foundations of the Western Intellectual Tradition 400–1400*. Yale University Press.

Crane, A., and Matten, D. (2004). Questioning the domain of the business ethics curriculum. *Journal of Business Ethics*, *54*(4), 357–369.

Crossan, M. M., Maurer, C. C., and White, R. E. (2011). Reflections on the 2009 AMR decade award: Do we have a theory of organizational learning? *Academy of Management Review*, *36*(3), 446–460.

Currie, J. K., and Newson, J. (Eds.). (1998). *Universities and Globalization: Critical Perspectives*. SAGE Publications.

Dahan, G., and Senol, I. (2012). Corporate social responsibility in higher education institutions: Istanbul Bilgi University case. *American International Journal of Contemporary Research*, *2*(3), 95–103.

Dahlsrud, A. (2008). How corporate social responsibility is defined: An analysis of 37 definitions. *Corporate Social Responsibility and Environmental Management*, *15*(1), 1–13.

Deem, R. (2001). Globalisation, new managerialism, academic capitalism and entrepreneurialism in universities: Is the local dimension still important? *Comparative Education*, *37*(1), 7–20.

Deem, R., and Brehony, K. J. (2005). Management as ideology: The case of "new managerialism" in higher education. *Oxford Review of Education*, *31*(2), 217–235.

Della Porta, D., Cini, L., and Guzman-Concha, C. (2020). *Contesting Higher Education: The Student Movements against Neoliberal Universities*. Policy Press.

den Heijer, A. C., and Curvelo Magdaniel, F. T. J. (2018). Campus–city relations: Past, present, and future. In P. Meusburger, M. Heffernan, and L. Suarsana (Eds.). *Geographies of the University* (pp. 439–459). Springer Open.

Devinney, T. M. (2009). Is the socially responsible corporation a myth? The good, the bad, and the ugly of corporate social responsibility. *The Academy of Management Perspectives*, *23*(2), 44–56.

DiMaggio, P. J. (1988). Interest and agency in institutional theory. In L. G. Zucker (Ed.). *Institutional Patterns and Organizations: Culture and Environment* (pp. 3–21). Ballinger.

DiMaggio, P. J., and Powell, W. W. (1983). The iron cage revisited: Institutional isomorphism and collective rationality in organizational fields. *American Sociological Review*, *48*(2), 147–160.

Djelic, M.-L. (2012). Scholars in the audit society: Understanding our contemporary iron cage. In L. Engwall (Ed.). *Scholars in Action: Past–Present–Future* (pp. 97–121). Acta Universitatis Upsaliensis.

Donoghue, F. (2018). *The Last Professors: The Corporate University and the Fate of the Humanities*. Fordham University Press.

Drori, G. S. (2005). *Global e-litism: Digital Technology, Social Inequality, and Transnationality*. Worth/Macmillan.

Drori, G. S. (2016). Professional consultancy and global higher education: The case of branding of academia. In A. Verger, C. Lubienski, and G. Steiner-Khamsi (Eds.). *The Global Education Industry (World Yearbook of Education 2016)* (pp. 175–189). Routledge.

Drori, G. S., and Meyer, J. W. (2006). Scientization: Making a world safe for organizing. In M.-L. Djelic and K. Sahlin-Andersson (Eds.). *Transnational Governance: Institutional Dynamics of Regulation* (pp. 31–52). Cambridge University Press.

Drori, G. S., Delmestri, G., and Oberg, A. (2013). Branding the university: Relational strategy of identity construction in a competitive field. In L. Engwall and P. Scott (Eds.). *Trust in Higher Education Institutions* (pp. 134–147). Portland Press.

Drori, G. S., Delmestri, G., and Oberg, A. (2016). The iconography of universities as institutional narratives. *Higher Education*, *71*(2), 163–180.

Drori, G. S., Meyer, J. W., and Hwang, H. (2006). *Globalization and Organization: World Society and Organizational Change*. Oxford University Press.

Drori, G. S., Meyer, J. W, Ramirez, F. O., and Schofer, A. (2003). *Science in the Modern World Polity: Institutionalization and Globalization.* Stanford University Press.

Duguid, P. (2005). "The art of knowing": Social and tacit dimensions of knowledge and the limits of the community of practice. *The Information Society*, *21*(2), 109–118.

Duryea, E. D., and Williams, D. T. (Eds.). (2013). *The Academic Corporation: A History of College and University Governing Boards*. Routledge.

Einstein, A. (1925). The mission of our university, *New Palestine*, 27 March 1925, 13, 294.

Enders, J., Kehm, B. M. and Schimank, U. (2015). Turning universities into actors on quasi-markets: How new public management reforms affect academic research. In D. Jansen and I. Pruisken (Eds.). *The Changing Governance of Higher Education and Research: Multilevel Perspectives* (pp. 89–103). Springer.

Engwall, L. (2008). The university: A multinational corporation. In L. Engwall and D. Weaire (Eds.). *The University in the Market* (pp. 9–21). Portland Press.

Etzkowitz, H. (2003). Innovation in innovation: The triple helix of university-industry-government relations. *Social Science Information*, *42*(3), 293–337.

Etzkowitz, H. (2008). *The Triple Helix: University–Industry–Government Innovation in Action*. Routledge.

Etzkowitz, H., and Leydesdorff, L. (2000). The dynamics of innovation: From national systems and "Mode 2" to a triple helix of university–industry–government relations. *Research Policy*, *29*(2), 109–123.
Eyal, G., and Bucholz, L. (2010). From the sociology of intellectuals to the sociology of interventions. *Annual Review of Sociology*, *36*, 117–137.
Factor, R., Oliver, A. L., and Montgomery, K. (2013). Beliefs about social responsibility at work: Comparisons between managers and non-managers over time and cross-nationally. *Business Ethics: A European Review*, *22*(2), 143–158.
Ferlie, E., Musselin, C., and Andresani, G. (2008). The steering of higher education systems: A public management perspective. *Higher Education*, *56*(3), 325–348.
Fleming, P., and Jones, M. T. (2013). *The End of Corporate Social Responsibility: Crisis and Critique*. SAGE Publications.
Frank, D. J., and Gabler, J. (2006). *Reconstructing the University: Worldwide Shifts in Academia in the 20th Century*. Stanford University Press.
Frank, D. J., and Meyer, J. W. (2007). University expansion and the knowledge society. *Theory and Society*, *36*(4), 287–311.
Frank, D. J., and Meyer, J. W. (2020). *The University and the Global Knowledge Society*. Princeton University Press.
Freeman, R. E., and Velamuri, S. R. (2006). A new approach to CSR: Company stakeholder responsibility. In A. Kakabadse (Ed.). *Corporate Social Responsibility* (pp. 9–23). Palgrave Macmillan.
Frickel, S., and Gross, N. (2005). A general theory of scientific/intellectual movements. *American Sociological Review*, *70*(2), 204–232.
Frost, J., Hattke, F., and Reihlen, M. (2016). Multi-level governance in universities: Strategy, structure, control. In J. Frost, F. Hattke, and M. Reihlen (Eds.). *Multi-level Governance in Universities* (pp. 1–15). Springer.
Galison, P. L., Holton, G., and Schweber, S. S. (Eds.). (2008). *Einstein for the 21st Century: His Legacy in Science, Art, and Modern Culture*. Princeton University Press.
Gallardo-Vázquez, D., and Sanchez-Hernandez, M. I. (2014). Measuring corporate social responsibility for competitive success at a regional level. *Journal of Cleaner Production*, *72*, 14–22.
Garriga, E., and Melé, D. (2004). Corporate social responsibility theories: Mapping the territory. *Journal of Business Ethics*, *53*(1–2), 51–71.
Gerber, L. G. (2014). *The Rise and Decline of Faculty Governance: Professionalization and the Modern American University*. JHU Press.
Geschwind, L., Jouni Kekäle, J., Pinheiro, R., and Sørensen, M. P. (2019). Responsible universities in context. In M. P. Sørensen, L. Geschwind, J. Kekäle, and R. Pinheiro (Eds.). *The Responsible University: Exploring the Nordic Context and Beyond* (pp. 3–38). Palgrave Macmillan.
Gherardi, S. (2011). Organizational learning: The sociology of practice. *Handbook of Organizational Learning and Knowledge Management*, *2*, 43–65.
Gibbons, M., Limoges, C., Nowotny, H., Schwartzman, S., Scott, P., and Trow, M. (1994). *The New Production of Knowledge: The Dynamics of Science and Research in Contemporary Societies*. SAGE Publications.

Ginwright, S., Cammarota, J., and Noguera, P. (2006). *Beyond Resistance! Youth Activism and Community Change: New Democratic Possibilities for Practice and Policy for America's Youth*. Routledge Taylor & Francis Group.

Gioia, D. A., and Corley, K. G. (2002). Being good versus looking good: Business school rankings and the Circean transformation from substance to image. *Academy of Management Learning & Education*, *1*(1), 107–120.

Grant, E. (1984). Science in the medieval university. In J. Kittleson and P. Transue (Eds.). *Rebirth, Reform and Resilience: Universities in Transition, 1300–1700* (pp. 68–102). Ohio State University Press.

Greenwald, R. (2007). The role of community-based clinical legal education in supporting public interest lawyering. *Harvard Civil Rights–Civil Liberties Law Review*, *42*, 569.

Greenwood, R., and Suddaby, R. (2006). Institutional entrepreneurship in mature fields: The big five accounting firms. *Academy of Management Journal*, *49*(1), 27–48.

Guenther, T. W. (2019). Third mission: A challenge for scholars? An editorial. *Journal of Management Control*, *30*, 247–249.

Gulbrandsen, M., and Smeby, J. C. (2005). Industry funding and university professors' research performance. *Research Policy*, *34*(6), 932–950.

Gutfreund, H. (2008). Einstein's Jewish identity. In A. Galison, B. Holton, and C. Schweber (Eds.). *Einstein for the 21st Century: His Legacy in Science, Art, and Modern Culture* (pp. 27–34). Princeton University Press.

Harré, N. (2007). Community service or activism as an identity project for youth. *Journal of Community Psychology*, *35*(6), 711–724.

Hladchenko, M., and Pinheiro, R. (2019). Implementing the triple helix model: Means–ends decoupling at the state level? *Minerva*, *57*(1), 1–22.

Holmwood, J. (Ed.). (2011). *A Manifesto for the Public University*. Bloomsbury.

Horta, H. (2009). Global and national prominent universities: Internationalization, competitiveness and the role of the State. *Higher Education*, *58*(3), 387–405.

Huisman, J., de Boer, H., and Goedegebuure, L. (2006). The perception of participation in executive governance structures in Dutch universities. *Tertiary Education & Management*, *12*(3), 227–239.

Jarrett, R. L., Sullivan, P. J., and Watkins, N. D. (2005). Developing social capital through participation in organized youth programs: Qualitative insights from three programs. *Journal of Community Psychology*, *33*(1), 41–55.

Jenkins, H. (2004). A critique of conventional CSR theory: An SME perspective. *Journal of General Management*, *29*(4), 37–57.

Jerome, F., and Taylor, R. (2005). *Einstein on Race and Racism*. Rutgers University Press.

Jongbloed, B., Enders, J., and Salerno, C. (2008). Higher education and its communities: Interconnections, interdependencies and a research agenda. *Higher Education*, *56*(3), 303–324.

Kallio, K.-M., Kallio, T. J., Tienari, J., and Hyvönen, T. (2016). Ethos at stake: Performance management and academic work in universities. *Human Relations*, *69*(3), 685–709.

Kaplin, W. A., and Lee, B. A. (2011). *The Law of Higher Education*. John Wiley & Sons.

Kaufman-Osborn, T. (2017). Disenchanted professionals: The politics of faculty governance in the neoliberal academy. *Perspectives on Politics*, *15*(1), 100–115.
Kennedy, M. D. (2014). *Globalizing Knowledge: Intellectuals, Universities, and Publics in Transformation*. Stanford University Press.
Kerr, C. (1963/2001). *The Uses of the University*. Harvard University Press.
King, R. (2009). *Governing Universities Globally: Organizations, Regulation and Rankings*. Edward Elgar Publishing.
Kipping, M., Üsdiken, B., and Puig, N. (2004). Imitation, tension, and hybridization: Multiple "Americanizations" of management education in Mediterranean Europe. *Journal of Management Inquiry*, *13*(2), 98–108.
Knorr-Cetina, K. (2009). *Epistemic Cultures: How the Sciences make Knowledge*. Harvard University Press.
Kosmützky, A., and Krücken, G. (2015). Sameness and difference: Analyzing institutional and organizational specificities of universities through mission statements. *International Studies of Management & Organization*, *45*(2), 137–149.
Kövér, Á., and Franger, G. (Eds.). (2019). *University and Society: Interdependencies and Exchange*. Edward Elgar Publishing.
Kretz, A., and Sá, C. (2013). Third stream, fourth mission: Perspectives on university engagement with economic relevance. *Higher Education Policy*, *26*(4), 497–506.
Krücken, G. (2003). Mission impossible? Institutional barriers to the diffusion of the "third academic mission" at German universities. *International Journal of Technology Management*, *25*(1–2), 18–33.
Krücken, G., and Meier, F. (2006). Turning the university into an organizational actor. In G. S. Drori, J. W. Meyer, and H. Hwang (Eds.). *Globalization and Organization: World Society and Organizational Change* (pp. 241–257). Oxford University Press.
Krücken, G., Kosmützky, A., and Torka, M. (2006). *Towards a Multiversity? Universities between Global Trends and National Traditions*. Verlag.
Krücken, G., Meier, F., and Müller, A. (2007). Information, cooperation, and the blurring of boundaries: Technology transfer in German and American discourses. *Higher Education*, *53*(6), 675–696.
Krücken, G., Meier, F., and Müller, A. (2009). Linkages to the civil society as "leisure time activities"? Experiences at a German university. *Science and Public Policy*, *36*(2), 139–144.
Lamont, M. (2009). *How Professors Think: Inside the Curious World of Academic Judgment*. Harvard University Press.
Lane, J. E., and Kinser, K. (2011). Reconsidering privatization in cross-border engagements: The sometimes public nature of private activity. *Higher Education Policy*, *24*(2), 255–273.
Laredo, P. (2007). Revisiting the third mission of universities: Toward a renewed categorization of university activities? *Higher Education Policy*, *20*(4), 441–456.
Leonardi, R., Nanetti, R. Y., and Putnam, R. D. (2001). *Making Democracy Work: Civic Traditions in Modern Italy*. Princeton University Press.

Levin, M., and Greenwood, D. J. (2016). *Creating a New Public University and Reviving Democracy: Action Research in Higher Education*. Berghahn Books.
Løvlie, L., and Standish, P. (2002). Introduction: Bildung and the idea of a liberal education. *Journal of Philosophy of Education*, *36*(3), 317–340.
Macfarlane, B. (2006). *The Academic Citizen: The Virtue of Service in University Life*. Routledge.
Macfarlane, B. (2013). *Intellectual Leadership in Higher Education: Renewing the Role of the University Professor*. Routledge.
Malik, M. (2015). Value-enhancing capabilities of CSR: A brief review of contemporary literature. *Journal of Business Ethics*, *127*(2), 419–438.
Margins, S. (2011). Higher education and the public good. *Higher Education Quarterly*, *65*(4), 411–433.
Marginson, S. (2006). Dynamics of national and global competition in higher education. *Higher Education*, *52*(1), 1–39.
Marginson, S. (2007). University mission and identity for a post post-public era. *Higher Education Research & Development*, *26*(1), 117–131.
Marginson, S., and Considine, M. (2000). *The Enterprise University: Power, Governance and Reinvention in Australia*. Cambridge University Press.
Matten, D., and Moon, J. (2008). "Implicit" and "explicit" CSR: A conceptual framework for a comparative understanding of corporate social responsibility. *Academy of Management Review*, *33*(2), 404–424.
Mazza, C., Quattrone, P., and Riccaboni, A. (Eds.). (2008). *European Universities in Transition: Issues, Models and Cases*. Edward Elgar Publishing.
McKeon, P. R. (1964). The status of the University of Paris as Parens scientiarum: An episode in the development of its autonomy. *Speculum*, *39*(4), 651–675.
Meyer, J. W., Ramirez, F. O., Frank, D. J., and Schofer, E. (2007). Higher education as an institution. In P. J. Gumport (Ed.). *Sociology of Higher Education: Contributions and their Contexts* (pp. 187–221). Johns Hopkins University Press.
Miller, D. C. (1963). Town and gown: The power structure of a university town. *American Journal of Sociology*, *68*(4), 432–443.
Mokyr, J. (2002). *The Gifts of Athena: Historical Origins of the Knowledge Economy*. Princeton University Press.
Montgomery, K., and Oliver, A. L. (2007). A fresh look at how professions take shape: Dual-directed networking dynamics and social boundaries. *Organization Studies*, *28*(5), 661–687.
Morsing, M., and Schultz, M. (2006). Corporate social responsibility communication: Stakeholder information, response and involvement strategies. *Business Ethics: A European Review*, *15*(4), 323–338.
Mowery, D. C., Nelson, R. R., Sampat, B. N., and Ziedonis, A. A. (2004). *Ivory Tower and Industrial Innovation: University–Industry Technology Transfer Before and After the Bayh–Dole Act*. Stanford University Press.
Muijen, H. S. C. A. (2004). Corporate social responsibility starts at university. *Journal of Business Ethics*, *53*(1–2), 235–246.
Murcia, M. J., Rocha, H. O., and Birkinshaw, J. (2018). Business schools at the crossroads? A trip back from Sparta to Athens. *Journal of Business Ethics*, *150*(2), 579–591.

Murray, K. B., and Vogel, C. M. (1997). Using a hierarchy-of-effects approach to gauge the effectiveness of corporate social responsibility to generate goodwill toward the firm: Financial versus nonfinancial impacts. *Journal of Business Research*, *38*(2), 141–159.

Musselin, C. (2007). Are universities specific organisations? In G. Krücken, C. Castor, A. Kosmützky, and M. Torka (Eds.). *Towards a Multiversity? Universities between Global Trends and National Traditions* (pp. 63–84). Verlag.

Musselin, C. (2013). *The Long March of French Universities*. Routledge.

Nedeva, M. (2007). New tricks and old dogs? The third mission and the re-production of the university. In R. D. Epstein, R. Boden, R. Deem, F. Rizvi, and S. Wright (Eds.). *Geographies of Knowledge, Geometries of Power: Higher Education in the 21st Century* (pp. 85–105). Routledge.

Nelson, R. R. (2001). Observations on the post-Bayh–Dole rise of patenting at American universities. *Journal of Technology Transfer*, *26*(1–2), 13.

Nowotny, H., Scott, P. B., and Gibbons, M. T. (2001). *Re-thinking Science: Knowledge and the Public in an Age of Uncertainty*. Polity Press.

Nyborg, P. (2003). Higher education as a public good and a public responsibility. *Higher Education in Europe*, *28*(3), 355–359.

Oliver, A. L. (2004). On the duality of competition and collaboration: Network-based knowledge relations in the biotechnology industry. *Scandinavian Journal of Management*, *20*(1–2), 151–171.

Oliver, A. L., and Liebeskind, J. P. (2009). Science and discoveries in the context of private and public knowledge creation and learning. In A. L. Oliver (Ed.). *Networks for Learning and Knowledge Creation in Biotechnology* (pp. 115–129). Cambridge University Press.

Oliver, A. L., and Montgomery, K. (2008). Using field-configuring events for sense-making: A cognitive network approach. *Journal of Management Studies*, *45*(6), 1147–1167.

O'Riordan, L., and Fairbrass, J. (2008). Corporate social responsibility (CSR): Models and theories in stakeholder dialogue. *Journal of Business Ethics*, *83*(4), 745–758.

Ortega y Gasset, J. (1946/2002). *Mission of the University* (H. L. Nostrand and C. Kerr, Trans.). Routledge.

Owen-Smith, J., and Powell, W. W. (2004). Knowledge networks as channels and conduits: The effects of spillovers in the Boston biotechnology community. *Organization Science*, *15*(1), 5–21.

Palfreyman, D., and Tapper, T. (2014). *Reshaping the University: The Rise of the Regulated Market in Higher Education*. Oxford University Press.

Pawłowski, K. (2009). The "fourth generation university" as a creator of the local and regional development. *Higher Education in Europe*, *34*(1), 51–64.

Perkmann, M., Tartari, V., McKelvey, M., Autio, E., Broström, A., D'Este, P., Fini, R., Geuna, A., Grimaldi, R., Hughes, A., Krabel, S., Kitson, M., Llerena, P., Lissoni, F., Salter, A., and Sobrero, M. (2013). Academic engagement and commercialisation: A review of the literature on university–industry relations. *Research Policy*, *42*(2), 423–442.

Phillips, N., Lawrence, T. B., and Hardy, C. (2000). Inter-organizational collaboration and the dynamics of institutional fields. *Journal of Management Studies*, *37*(1), 23–43.

Pinheiro, R., and Stensaker, B. (2014). Designing the entrepreneurial university: The interpretation of a global idea. *Public Organization Review*, *14*(4), 497–516.

Pinheiro, R., Benneworth, P., and Jones, G. A. (Eds.). (2012). *Universities and Regional Development: A Critical Assessment of Tensions and Contradictions*. Routledge.

Pinheiro, R., Langa, P. V., and Pausits, A. (2015). One and two equals three? The third mission of higher education institutions. *European Journal of Higher Education*, *5*(3), 233–249.

Polletta, F., and Jasper, J. M. (2001). Collective identity and social movements. *Annual Review of Sociology*, *27*(1), 283–305.

Pope, S., Bromley, P., Lim, A., and Meyer, J. W. (2018). The pyramid of nonprofit responsibility: The institutionalization of organizational responsibility across sectors. *VOLUNTAS: International Journal of Voluntary and Nonprofit Organizations*, *29*(6), 1300–1314.

Pope, S., and Wæraas, A. (2016). CSR-washing is rare: A conceptual framework, literature review, and critique. *Journal of Business Ethics*, *137*(1), 173–193.

Press, E., and Washburn, J. (2000). The kept university. *Atlantic Monthly*, *285*(3), 39–54.

Putnam, R. D. (2000). *Bowling Alone: The Collapse and Revival of American Community*. Simon & Schuster.

Quinn, J. B. (1999). Strategic outsourcing: Leveraging knowledge capabilities. *MIT Sloan Management Review*, *40*(4), 9.

Quinn, J. B., Anderson, P., and Finkelstein, S. (1996). Leveraging intellect. *Academy of Management Perspectives*, *10*(3), 7–27.

Raines, J. P., and Leathers, C. G. (2003). *The Economic Institutions of Higher Education: Economic Theories of University Behaviour*. Edward Elgar Publishing.

Ramakrishna, S., Ngowi, A., De Jager, H., and Awuzie, B. O. (2020). Emerging industrial revolution: Symbiosis of industry 4.0 and circular economy: The role of universities. *Science, Technology and Society*, DOI 10.1177/0971721820912918.

Ramirez, F. O., and Christensen, T. (2013). The formalization of the university: Rules, roots, and routes. *Higher Education*, *65*(6), 695–708.

Ramirez, F. O., and Meyer, J. W. (2013). Universalizing the university in a world society. In J. Cheol Shin and B. M. Kehm (Eds.). *Institutionalization of World-class University in Global Competition* (pp. 257–273). Springer.

Ramirez, F. O., Luo, X., Schofer, E., and Meyer, J. W. (2006). Student achievement and national economic growth. *American Journal of Education*, *113*(1), 1–29.

Rhoades, G., and Stensaker, B. (2017). Bringing organisations and systems back together: Extending Clark's entrepreneurial university. *Higher Education Quarterly*, *71*(2), 129–140.

Rhoten, D., and Powell, W. W. (2007). The frontiers of intellectual property: Expanded protection versus new models of open science. *The Annual Review of Law and Social Science*, 3(1), 345–373.
Rhoten, D. R., and Powell, W. W. (2010). Public research universities: From land grant to federal grant to patent grant institutions. In D. Rhoten and C. Calhoun (Eds.). *Knowledge Matters* (pp. 319–345). Columbia University Press.
Riddle, P. (1993). Political authority and university formation in Europe, 1200–1800. *Sociological Perspectives*, 36(1), 45–62.
Rosenkranz, Z. (2011). The "botched university": Einstein's involvement in the Hebrew university, 1924–1929. In A. Goren (Ed.). *Einstein before Israel: Zionist Icon or Iconoclast?* (pp. 181–207). Princeton University Press.
Rosenkranz, Z. E., and Wolff, B. (2007). *Einstein: The Persistent Illusion of Transience.* Magnes Press.
Rotblat, J. (Ed.). (1982). *Proceedings of the First Pugwash Conference on Science and World Affairs, Pugwash Council, 1982*, 167–170.
Rotblat, J. (Ed.). (1997/2016). *World Citizenship*. Springer.
Rowe, D. E., and Schulman, R. J. (Eds.). (2007). *Einstein in Politics: His Private Thoughts and Public Stands on Nationalism*. Princeton University Press.
Rüegg, W. (1992). Foreword. In H. de Ridder-Symoens (Ed.). *The History of the University in Europe (Vol I): Universities in the Middle Ages* (pp. xix–xxvi). Cambridge University Press.
Sahlin, K., Wijkström, F., Dellmuth, L., Einarsson, T., and Oberg, A. (2015). The "Milky Way" of intermediary organisations: A transnational field of university governance. *Policy & Politics*, 43(3), 407–424.
Sammalisto, K., and Arvidsson, K. (2005). Environmental management in Swedish higher education: Directives, driving forces, hindrances, environmental aspects and environmental co-ordinators in Swedish universities. *International Journal of Sustainability in Higher Education*, 6(1), 18–35.
Schimank, U. (2005). "New public management" and the academic profession: Reflections on the German situation. *Minerva*, 43(4), 361–376.
Schofer, E., and Meyer, J. W. (2005). The worldwide expansion of higher education in the twentieth century. *American Sociological Review*, 70(6), 898–920.
Schwartz, L. E. (1967). Perspective on Pugwash. *International Affairs (Royal Institute of International Affairs 1944–)*, 43(3), 498–515.
Serrano-Velarde, K., and Krücken, G. (2012). Private sector consultants and public universities: The challenges of cross-sectoral knowledge transfers. *European Journal of Education*, 47(2), 277–289.
Setó-Pamies, D., Domingo-Vernis, M., and Rabassa-Figueras, N. (2011). Corporate social responsibility in management education: Current status in Spanish universities. *Journal of Management and Organization*, 17(5), 604.
Shore, C., and McLauchlan, L. (2012). "Third mission" activities, commercialisation and academic entrepreneurs. *Social Anthropology*, 20(3), 267–286.
Shurkin, J. N. (2006). *Broken Genius: The Rise and Fall of William Shockley, Creator of the Electronic Age*. Palgrave Macmillan.
Slaughter, S. (2001). Academic freedom, professional autonomy, and the state. In J.C. Hermanowicz (Ed.). *American Academic Profession: Transformation*

*in Contemporary Higher Education*. (pp. 246–255). Johns Hopkins University Press.

Slaughter, S., and Rhoades, G. (2004). *Academic Capitalism and the New Economy: Markets, State, and Higher Education*. Johns Hopkins University Press.

Smelser, N. J. (2013). *Dynamics of the Contemporary University: Growth, Accretion, and Conflict*. University of California Press.

Stensaker, B. (2007). Quality as fashion: Exploring the translation of a management idea into higher education. In D. F. Westerheijden, B. Stensaker and M. J. Rosa (Eds.). *Quality Assurance in Higher Education* (pp. 99–118). Springer.

Stevens, M. L., Armstrong, E. A., and Arum, R. (2008). Sieve, incubator, temple, hub: Empirical and theoretical advances in the sociology of higher education. *Annual Review of Sociology*, *34*, 127–151.

Tapper, E. R., and Salter, B. G. (1995). The changing idea of university autonomy. *Studies in Higher Education*, *20*(1), 59–71.

Theiss-Morse, E. (2009). *Who Counts as an American? The Boundaries of National Identity*. Cambridge University Press.

Thune, T., Reymert, I., Gulbrandsen, M., and Aamodt, P. O. (2016). Universities and external engagement activities: Particular profiles for particular universities? *Science and Public Policy*, *43*(6), 774–786.

Trencher, G., Yarime, M., McCormick, K. B., Doll, C. N. H., and Kraines, S. B. (2014). Beyond the third mission: Exploring the emerging university function of co-creation for sustainability. *Science and Public Policy*, *41*(2), 151–179.

Tuchman, G. (2009). *Wannabe U: Inside the Corporate University*. University of Chicago Press.

Verger, J. (1992). Patterns. In H. de Ridder-Symoens (Ed.). *The History of the University in Europe (Vol I): Universities in the Middle Ages* (pp. 35–76). Cambridge University Press.

Watermeyer, R. (2012a). From engagement to impact? Articulating the public value of academic research. *Tertiary Education and Management*, *18*(2), 115–130.

Watermeyer, R. (2012b). Issues in the articulation of "impact": UK academics' response to "impact" as a new measure of research assessment. *Studies in Higher Education*, *39*(2), 359–377.

Wedlin, L. (2006). *Ranking Business Schools: Forming Fields, Identities and Boundaries in International Management Education*. Edward Elgar Publishing.

Weick, K. E. (1979). *The Social Psychology of Organizing (Topics in Social Psychology Series)*. McGraw-Hill Humanities.

Wenger, E. (1998). Communities of practice: Learning as a social system. *Systems Thinker*, *9*(5), 2–3.

Wenger, E. (2000). Communities of practice and social learning systems. *Organization*, *7*(2), 225–246.

Wenger, E. (2010). Communities of practice and social learning systems: The career of a concept. In C. Blackmore (Ed.). *Social Learning Systems and Communities of Practice* (pp. 179–198). Springer.

Wenger, E. C., and Snyder, W. M. (2000). Communities of practice: The organizational frontier. *Harvard Business Review*, *78*(1), 139–146.

West, E. G. (1995/2018). The economics of higher education. In J. Sommer (Ed.). *The Academy in Crisis: Political Economy of Higher Education* (2nd ed.) (pp. 135–169). Routledge.

Williamson, O. E. (1981). The economics of organization: The transaction cost approach. *American Journal of Sociology*, *87*(3), 548–577.

Willmott, H. (1995). Managing the academics: Commodification and control in the development of university education in the UK. *Human Relations*, *48*(9), 993–1027.

Wissema, J. G. (2009). *Towards the Third Generation University: Managing the University in Transition*. Edward Elgar Publishing.

Wyatt, J. F. (1981). Ortega y Gasset's *Mission of the University*: An appropriate document for an age of economy? *Studies in Higher Education*, *6*(1), 59–69.

Zhang, L., Liu, J., and Zhang, J. (2018). The mission and responsibilities of innovative universities. *European Review*, *26*(2), 311–318.

# Index

academia/academicians 76
 history 65
 inside–outside role of 132
 leaders and managers 64
 "likeminded" 100
 publicness 20
 social role 59–60
academic/academy
 activities, social projects with 117–18
 autonomy 14, 28, 33, 132, 143
 based knowledge 118
 capitalism 27
 credentialing 19
 credit 67
 education 65
 governance, changes in 72
 knowledge 24
 labour 67, 144
 mission 15–16, 74–5
 performance 144
 programmes, internationalization of 54
 publications 30
 research 136
 responsibility 3
 scholars 98
 teaching 32, 74
academic commitment and leadership (ACL) 1–3, 64–5, 68, 100, 132–3, 145
 academia/academicians 35–6, 76–7, 142
 actions taken by universities 36, 136
 activities 137–8, 144
 advancement and protection of public good 93–8
 analytic categorization for 62

claims regarding 8
communities of practice see communities of practice
conception of 38
contemporary varieties 65–76
critiques 136–9
definition of 3–8, 38–9, 135
designated office for 136
dimensions of 61
Einstein see Einstein, A.
elements of 57
epistemic and ethical aspects of practice 113
examples for 121
exemplars 93
expansive review of 93
expectations towards 50
features to 40
goals and plans 141–2
Hoffman Leadership and Responsibility Programme 114–20
implementation 61
initiatives 134, 141
innovation and change of 138–9
institutional perspective to 55
and leadership 3
management of 135
mission of 136, 142
models of 36, 52, 61, 133
networks of practice 112–13
organizational process 39
perspective of 72
potency of 134
practices of 50, 55, 67, 69
principles 74
priorities for 141
projects 121, 142

quantification, bureaucratization, and rationalization of 144
role of 76–7
Russell–Einstein Manifesto 80–86
social engagement 143
standards of 71–2
strategies of 65, 67, 72
themes in university 74
theoretical understanding of 49
tiers of 139–40
trends of 36
university's adoption of 133
university's integrity and strategic understanding of 135–6
valorization strategies 72
varieties of 73
academic freedom
norm of 141
of study 69
academic mission 6–7, 9, 23–4, 26
fourth 34–7
of teaching 74–5
of universities 72–4
academic missions
"traditional" 72
academic revolution 21–9
ACL *see* academic commitment and leadership (ACL)
actionable leadership 139
activism 76, 78, 98, 145
administrative reforms 32
Advisory Committee on Uranium 85
African Americans 77
rights of 78
anti-Communism 81–4
antisemitism 88
artefacts 109
artificial intelligence (AI) 71
Ashridge Model of vision–mission–goals 89
Athenian paradigm 75
autonomy 20–21, 52, 66, 141
intellectual 22
norm of 141
operational 22

against utility and engagement 132

beneficiaries 16
*Beyond the Ivory Tower* (Bok) 12
*Bildung* philosophical tradition 19
Biligi University, Istanbul 97
*bios praktikos* 22
*bios theoretikos* 22
Bok, D. 6, 12
Bologna Declaration of 1988 86
Bologna proclamation 89–90
bottom-up 4, 38, 58, 64, 72, 76, 96, 98, 100, 144
Bourdieu, P. 132
Bozeman, B. 19–20
brokerage 5
Bush, V. 2

Campbell, J. L. 43, 48–51
Carroll, A. B. 41, 139
pyramid model of CSR 42
cathedrals of earning 27
cathedrals of learning 27
chauvinism 87
circular economy 70–71
city university partnerships 66
civil rights 78–9
promotion of 139
Clark, B. 27, 143
cohesive group of practices 107
commercialization 7, 72, 136
of inventions 24
commercial returns 18
commitment 139, 146
academic 3
knowledge and 123
and leadership 70
public 14, 17–21
social 13–17, 121–2, 145
as strategy 139–40
*see also* academic commitment and leadership (ACL)
Communism 81–4
communities of practice 100–103
activities 108
artefacts 109

concept of 101
connectivity 105–7
and group boundaries 109–12
leadership 104–5
learning projects 108–9
membership 107–8
paradigmatic conceptualization of 110
public events 103–4
community activities 96
community-based learning 109–10, 120
community-based public events 103–4
community-based social activities 118
community-related artefacts 109
comparative political economy 48
competences 110–11
definition of 101
"social containers" of 101
connectedness 112
contemporary academia 138–9
issues for 141
contemporary universities 29
coronavirus global pandemic, public engagement during 145–6
corporate for-profit organizations 134
corporate social responsibility (CSR) 5, 38, 40, 132–3
for academia 54–6
to ACL 56–9
analytical frameworks of 47
basic elements of 56
charges levied against 134
core-skeleton component of 43
and critical accounts from within paradigm 48–9
critiques levied against 134
definition of 41, 44–5, 139
diffusion of practices 55–6
discourse of 139
economic conditions 49–50
elements of 57
for-profit practice of 133
global adaptations of 52
imprint of 70
initiatives 137
institutional conditions 50–51
legacy of 40–42, 134
models of 42–6
and new public management in 51–3
organized acts of 134
proposition on 50
pyramid model of 42, 139
range of perceptions of 43
reformulation of 53
reliable measures of 43
spirit of 57
stakeholders' role in 46–7
strategies 53
theoretical approach to 48
theory of 41
translation from 40
critical thinking 94
capabilities 95
Crossan, M. M. 58–9
CSR *see* corporate social responsibility (CSR)
culture 72

Dahan, G. 53
degree of self-awareness 102
degrees of intentionality 65
Della Porta, D. 27
democratic decision-making process 105
distance learning 74
diversity of partners 141
Djelic, M.-L. 23–4, 34
doctoral degrees 7
"do no harm" investment strategy 70
Du Bois, W. E. B. 78
Duguid, P. 112

economic hardships 49
economic responsibility 41, 53
education system 36
effectiveness 112
EHEA *see* European Higher Education Area (EHEA)
Einstein, A. 15, 77, 88, 133–4
advocating for rights of African Americans 77–80

as role model for 92–3
social role 86
and "The Mission of Our
   University" 86–92
Emergency Committee of Atomic
   Scientists 86
employability 31
employee wellness 53
enterprise 102
   university 27
entrepreneurial initiatives 77
entrepreneurial managers 51
entrepreneurial university 25, 27, 34,
   61
environmental responsibility 52–3
epistemic ability 113
epistemic culture 112
equality 92
ethical investors 70
ethics, standards of 132
ethnicity empowerment 138
Etzkowitz, H. 25–6
European Commission 71
European Higher Education Area
   (EHEA) 89
expansiveness 112
extension activities 144

Factor, R. 43
Fairbrass, J. 62
family-friendly policies 119
fellowships 137–8
Ferlie, E. 51
financial fiduciary responsibilities 70
financial returns 18
flexible activities 119
Foreign Affairs and International
   Trade Canada 44
for-profit companies 51–2
Frank, D. J. 145
freedom 141
Freeman, R. E. 134–5

general practitioner/physician 122–3
Geschwind, L. 32
global cultural transformations 32
globalization 145

Google-specific technologies 29
Google Translate 29
governance
   authority 141
   networked mode of 25
   reforms 32
Granger, L. B. 79
greenhouse 9, 62, 94, 98
group
   bonding 116–17
   boundaries 109–12
   cohesion 106, 114
   learning 108, 111–12
   meetings 105, 116, 119
group membership 108–10
   achievements 117
   empowering 118

Harvard Management Company 69
Hebrew University of Jerusalem 63,
   67, 77, 86, 88, 97–8, 116–17,
   120, 122
higher education 56–7
   organizations 7
Hoffman Leadership and
   Responsibility Programme 63,
   103–4, 114, 116–17, 120, 121,
   134
Holmwood, J. 35
Horizon Impact Award 2, 71
human capital related returns 18
humanity 81
   nuclear threats to 85
Human Rights Watch 29–30
Humboldtian university model 23

identity 111–12
   project 145
industrial returns 18
informal meetings 117
innovation processes 24–5
innovative organizational change 59
institutional analysis 48–9
institutional entrepreneurs 76
institutional environment 52
institutional inspiration 139
institutionalization

of organizations 135–6
of practices 56
institutional resilience 146
institutional theory 48, 56
integration, universities
   as greenhouse of social
     leadership 94–7
   as institutions generating
     diffusion spillover 97–8
   as social integrators 93–4
intellectual autonomy 22
intellectual leaders 96
intellectual property (IP) 24
internal fellowships 115
internal group activities 112
internal leadership 104
Internet of Things (IoT) 71
IoT see Internet of Things (IoT)
IP see intellectual property (IP)
Israel 95
   college revolution 67
Israeli Council of Higher Education 138

Jewish exceptionalism 88
Jewish nationalism 87
Jewish university 23
justice, standards of 132
justification, distinct tradition of 17

Kerr, C. 12, 19, 24
Knorr-Cetina, K. 112
knowledge 22–4, 132
   commercialization 35, 75–6
   and commitment 123
   definition of 15
   development of 17
   economy 29
   exchange 113
   production 33, 75–6
   pursuit of 12
Krücken, G. 144

labour market 16, 30–31, 33
leadership 6, 96, 139–40, 146
   academic commitment and 3
   activities and practices 104
   initiatives 105
   internal 104
   qualities 104–5
   social responsibly and 95
   as strategy 139–40
   see also academic commitment
     and leadership (ACL)
learning
   meaningful 110
   modes of 33
   projects 108–9
   systems 110
leverage 4–5

managerialism 27, 133, 141
Manhattan Project 85
mankind 80
marketization 27, 33, 140, 141
market logics 27
medieval universities 21–2
Meyer, J. W. 145
military strategy, authorities in 82–3
mission drift 28
MIT 24–5
Montgomery, K. 111
Muijen, H. S. C. A. 53
multiplicity of social objectives 65
Murcia, M. J. 75
mutuality 101–2
mutual participation 101

nanotechnology 71
National Holocaust Institute 122
nationalism 87–8
networks of practice 112–13
Newcastle University 66
new public management (NPM)
   practices 51
   to universities 33
nonexclusive licensing 136
Novartis, research partnership 28
Nowotny, H. 33
NPM see new public management (NPM)

Oliver-Lumerman, A. 62, 111
ontological turn 34–7

Open University model 74
operational autonomy 22
Organisation for Economic Co-operation and Development (OECD) 29
O'Riordan, L. 62

partners 16
personal constraints 114–15
philanthropic responsibility 53
political censorship 31–2
political economy 48
political rights, promotion of 139
practice-based activities 112
Princeton University Investment Company (PRINCO) 69
PRINCO *see* Princeton University Investment Company (PRINCO)
private interests, specification and protection of 113
private organizations 19
private universities 20
process of sharing 113
proclamations 69
professional academic labour 68
professional autonomy 31
professionalism 141
programme's initial policy 119
projects 121–2
    community gardens for elderly citizens who emigrated from Ethiopia to Israel 129
    Education Law Clinic 127–8
    gender bias in choosing high school specialization 126–7
    in-house pharmacology expert advice to elderly people 122–3
    Jewish–Arabic collaborative reading sessions of religious writing 128–9
    needs of cows 124–5
    pro-peace social entrepreneurship 128

Revolution Orchestra 123–4
    Starcatcher Community Theatre in English 126
    Teaching Aids for Science and Technology (STS) Teachers 125
proprietary knowledge, ownership of 16–17
psychological counselling 68
public affairs 139–40
    leadership in 139
    universities engagement with 140
public agencies 146
public budgets 18
public commitment 13–14, 17–21
public engagement during coronavirus global pandemic 145–6
public events 103–4
public goods 13, 19, 56, 75, 139, 146
    responsibility for 64, 133
public interest centres 67–8
public lectures 144
publicness 19–20
public organizations 19
Pugwash movement 80–81
Putnam, R. D. 36

raw material of emergence 58
recipients 16
registration of patents 144
reliant 5–6
repertoires 102
    "translating" 111
research-driven technology 76
resource availability 104
responsibility 14
Russell, B. 80
Russell–Einstein Manifesto 68, 80–86

scholarship 22–3
scholars, professional community of 143
scientific norms 141
scientific scholars 96
SDGs *see* Sustainable Development Goals (SDGs)
second academic revolution 25

self-awareness 102
self-reflection 141
self-regulation 51, 64
Senol, I. 53
sense of knowing 111–12
service-oriented culture 33
shared repertoire 102
sharing
   personal identities 112
   process of 113
Shockley, W. 68
Silicon Valley, semiconductor industry of 68
Slaughter, S. 27
social actions, authenticity of 136
social activism 76
social advocacy 78
social bonding 114
social capital 102
social change 3, 64, 68
   academic leadership towards 72
   leadership of 72
   projects of 96
social commitment 121–2, 145
   ontology of 13–17
social containers of competences 101
social engagement 64, 144–5
   vision and strategy for 143
social entrepreneurship 96
social gathering 101
social groups 122
   boundaries of 111
social impact 15–16
   academic tradition of 64
social institutions 64, 97
social integration 78–9, 92–4
socialization 107
social justice 92
social leadership 94–7
social missions 56
social policy, alternative options for 94
social programmes 75
social resources, distribution of 18
social responsibility 13–14, 44, 49, 55–6, 108, 114
   actions of 95
   activities of 49–50, 98
   institutionalization of 13
   and leadership 95
   practices 50, 56
social segregation 93–4
social services 68
social situations 93
societal challenges 134
   complexity of 141
societal welfare 34–5
society, normative beliefs and prospects of 15
sovereignty 139–40
Spartan paradigm 75
stakeholders 16, 39, 41–3, 51, 142
   expansion and variety of 143
   features and composition of 143
   in institutional environment 143
   involvement 64
   role in CSR 46–7
Stanford Management Company 69
Stanford University 136
state bureaucracy 94
Sustainable Development Goals (SDGs) 2, 71
synergies 118

tacit knowledge, importance of 113
teaching 59
   academic mission of 74–5
   modes of 33
   primary mission of 23
technology transfer 7, 24
"The Mission of Our University" 86–92
*The Uses of the University* (Kerr) 12
"third party" organizations 71
time constraints 116
*Times Higher Education* (THE) journal 71
town and gown 65–6, 133
"traditional" academic missions 72
transaction costs 113
transition 107
translation 39–40
   repertoires 111
Transparency International 29

triangle of coordination 143
triple helix model 24–5
true universities 89–90

Umschweif, G. 122
unconferences 106
universities 12–13, 24–5, 38–40
    academic mission of 72–4
    academic study of 144–5
    ACL 59–63, 141
    amassing resources 69
    aspects of 54
    autonomy 54
    changing institution of 36
    commitment and leadership of 70
    compliance of 71–2
    criticism of 34
    CSR *see* corporate social responsibility (CSR)
    engagement 61
    engagement with public affairs 140
    epochal models of 1–2
    features of 55
    focus on commercialization 133
    fourth academic mission 34–7
    governance 142–3
    historiography of 21–8
    history of 15
    institution of 145–6
    knowledge 27
    millennium-old organizational form of 12
    missions of 22, 24, 26–7, 33, 100, 134
    modern-day 66
    new public management (NPM) to 33
    non-commercial engagement of 8
    ontology of social commitment 13–17
    persistence of institution of 12
    practice of 89
    proactive engagement of 61
    programmatic tool for 141
    programmes 5–6
    proliferation of 1
    *vs.* public commitment 17–21
    public role of 6, 12, 17–18, 132
    schematic differentiation between 35
    signs of 145–6
    social impact of 60, 71
    social mission 57
    social role of 2, 12–13, 16
    third academic revolution 28–34
    worldwide response of 145–6
university-based clinics 68
university–society relations 132–4
    ACL as reflection on the character of universities 141–5
    commitment and leadership as strategy 139–40
    CSR 134–9
    history of 132–3
    public engagement during coronavirus global pandemic 145–6
urban development 66

valorization
    practices 71
    strategies 72
Velamuri, S. R. 134–5
visualization 139–40
volunteering 108
volunteering projects 121, 126, 136, 138
von Humboldt, W. 23

WBCSD *see* World Business Council on Sustainable Development (WBCSD)
weapons of mass destruction 81–2
Weick, K. E. 59
Wenger, E. 101–3, 109, 111
    group boundaries 111
World Bank 29
World Business Council on Sustainable Development (WBCSD) 43–4